P9-CQY-399

"Nicole's kindness truly is contagious, but the really good news is that yours can be too. If we take *The Negativity Remedy* to heart, what a wonderfully more joy-filled world it will be!"

Bob Goff, *New York Times* bestselling author of *Love Does* and *Everybody Always*

"*The Negativity Remedy* is a must-read if you sometimes need help dealing with difficult people. If everyone took Nicole's messages of kindness to heart, what a joyful difference it would make in the world!"

Ken Blanchard, coauthor of *The New One Minute Manager*® and *Servant Leadership in Action*

"I picked up this book and within minutes knew I'd found the insight I had been looking for. Nicole uses her past struggles and hilarious insights to help us understand that kindness is contagious. If you have even one doubt about yourself or the direction of your life, run to the register with *The Negativity Remedy*. It's a winner!"

Lu Parker, Emmy Award–winning TV news anchor and founder of Be Kind & Co.

"Nicole Phillips has written the definitive how-to guide for everyone wanting to make kindness an intentional part of their lives. Read *The Negativity Remedy* and learn from this brave author on the frontlines of the kindness culture."

Dr. Neal Nybo, motivational speaker, trainer, pastor, and author

"Filled with humor, insight, and refreshing honesty, *The Negativity Remedy* offers a beautiful way to live. Nicole's empowering message shows up in everyday moments to create real, attainable change. A fantastic book for us all!"

Lisa Barrickman, author of *A Case for Kindness: 40 Ways to Love and Inspire Others*

"This lovely book will show you how to erase the negativity in your life and replace it with compassion, connection, and courage. With delicious humor and fresh insight, Nicole Phillips shows how we can transform our perceptions—and our lives—through kindness. Not sterile, goody-goody kindness, but authentic, messy, and oh-so-powerful kindness! Give yourself and your friends the gift of *The Negativity Remedy*!"

Donna Cameron, author of *A Year of Living Kindly*

the
Negativity
Remedy

Unlocking More Joy,
Less Stress, and Better Relationships
through Kindness

Nicole J. Phillips

BakerBooks

a division of Baker Publishing Group
Grand Rapids, Michigan

© 2020 by Nicole J. Phillips

Published by Baker Books
a division of Baker Publishing Group
PO Box 6287, Grand Rapids, MI 49516-6287
www.bakerbooks.com

Printed in the United States of America

All rights reserved. No part of this publication may be reproduced, stored in a retrieval system, or transmitted in any form or by any means—for example, electronic, photocopy, recording—without the prior written permission of the publisher. The only exception is brief quotations in printed reviews.

Library of Congress Cataloging-in-Publication Data
Names: Phillips, Nicole J., 1975– author.
Title: The negativity remedy : unlocking more joy, less stress, and better relationships through kindness / Nicole J. Phillips.
Description: Grand Rapids, Michigan : Baker Books, a division of Baker Publishing Group, 2020.
Identifiers: LCCN 2020003188 | ISBN 9781540900104 (paperback)
Subjects: LCSH: Kindness—Religious aspects—Christianity. | Interpersonal relations—Religious aspects—Christianity.
Classification: LCC BV4647.K5 P475 2020 | DDC 248.4—dc23
LC record available at https://lccn.loc.gov/2020003188

Scripture quotations are from the *Holy Bible*, New Living Translation, copyright © 1996, 2004, 2007, 2013, 2015 by Tyndale House Foundation. Used by permission of Tyndale House Publishers, Inc., Carol Stream, Illinois 60188. All rights reserved.

The author is represented by WordServe Literary Group, www.wordserveliterary.com.

Some names and details have been changed to protect the privacy of the individuals involved.

20   21   22   23   24   25   26   7   6   5   4   3   2

In keeping with biblical principles of creation stewardship, Baker Publishing Group advocates the responsible use of our natural resources. As a member of the Green Press Initiative, our company uses recycled paper when possible. The text paper of this book is composed in part of post-consumer waste.

I dedicate this book to my mom,

the first person to teach me about the power of kindness.

Contents

Introduction   9

1. Lessons from Dinoland 15

2. Identifying Your Inner Meanie   23

3. What Actual Experts Are Saying about Kindness   33

4. Drawing More Kindness into Your Life: *Saying Yes to the Positive*   47

5. Saying No to the Negative   61

6. What Counts as Kindness: *Are People Taking Advantage of You?*   73

7. When Kindness Isn't about You   83

8. Being Kind in Your Home and Other Places Where People Annoy You   93

9. Being Kind to People Who Hurt You   105

10. When Kindness Can't Fix It   115

Contents

11. When Good Acts of Kindness Go Bad   123

12. Why Kindness Even Matters   133

Acknowledgments   139

365 Kindness Ideas   141

Author Q & A   165

Notes   169

Introduction

My bestie, Andrea, has commented over the past several years about how kind I am, how easily kindness and compassion seem to come to me. She's not complimenting me. She's perplexed. Andrea has known me long enough to have had a front row seat to the transformation kindness has caused in my life. She is the one person (aside from my husband) who knows just how big my inner meanie can be—she's been insulted and beaten down by my inner meanie, and yet we remain besties. Therefore, I get it. Andrea has every right to say, "What happened here?"

I used to drink like a fish. When I wasn't an absolutely hysterical drunk, I had a tendency to get mouthy and, well, mean.

One night I went to a bar without my husband because I was angry with him for traveling so much. He's a college basketball coach, so of course he travels a lot. I wasn't surprised by it; I was just sick of it. I proceeded to drink so much that when a man tried to lure me into his car, I didn't even realize I was in jeopardy of being abducted. Everything turned out just fine; a girlfriend jumped in before I got hurt. But yes, the memory of that night and what could have happened still haunts me sometimes. And it all started because I handed the car keys to my inner meanie.

You'd think that would have been enough to curb my enthusiasm for rum and cokes, but it wasn't.

About a year later, I was with my husband at a campus bar when I started in on all his little flaws. It began as a joke that only my inner meanie found funny, and it ended in a display of public embarrassment for all involved.

The next morning, I was lying on the carpet of my bedroom floor when my husband walked into our room. He simply and clearly stated, "You owe me an apology." I knew I owed him a whole lot more than that. I owed my husband and my children and everyone I loved a whole lot more than that. It was clear that something needed to change.

I never took another drink again.

Stone-cold sober, but high on life, I traded in thoughts about when my next drink was coming for a daily journey with kindness. I stumbled upon the idea of using kindness to retrain my brain, thanks to a girl in fashionable boots, but you'll have to wait until chapter 1 to hear about her. Now, don't let me fool you into thinking I just did an act of kindness every time I wanted to have a drink. It wasn't that easy. There were a lot of things my husband and I had to rework in our relationship for me to get healthy. I spent a lot of time in the bathtub learning what it means to relax while he read bedtime stories to our kids. Instead of staying up late laughing and watching TV together, I went to bed at nine o'clock or whenever the urge to drink hit hardest. Eventually, I stumbled upon a secret: my drinking wasn't really about outside influences, stress levels, or the way people were treating me. Neither was my overall level of joy. It was about me. It was all determined by the lens through which I chose to see life.

When I got an unexpected bill in the mail, when my husband had to work late, or when my toddler was whinier than usual, my first thought was, *I cannot wait to have a drink.* I knew that drink would allow me to finally relax. I would be free from the world, because the world was the problem, right? Wrong. The drinking seemed like it was about other people, but it wasn't. It was about me. I had to get to the point where I realized my drinking had nothing to do with external circumstances but instead had everything to do with how I was processing those situations. It was about my inability to see the good around me because I was so set in my ways of looking at everything as a negative. Even if you're not an alcoholic, placing the blame on the world creates a pathway of negativity in our lives. Luckily, there is a remedy. It's kindness. Once we learn to understand and use kindness to our advantage, the game changes. We begin to recognize kindness isn't about other people; it's about us. We help someone else when we give them a few dollars or a word of encouragement, but the life we *transform* with kindness is our own.

I began writing a weekly column called "Kindness Is Contagious" for newspapers in North Dakota and Minnesota. The thing about writing a weekly column is that you have to write it weekly. Like every week. I asked readers to send in their stories of kindness and how it made them feel to give or receive that kindness, but if my inbox was empty I still had to meet my deadline. The journalist in me was set on high alert for any potential material. I began noticing opportunities to help people out, and I became ultra-aware of when people were helping me.

Very quickly, my inner meanie was silenced and my brain was retrained to see the good in the world. Within one year of being intentional about kindness, I quit drinking, quit smoking, stopped gossiping, lost thirty pounds, and re-fell in love with my husband. Yep, I was high on life. Still am.

Do you ever feel like something is missing? Like true joy is so close and yet just out of reach? I lived in that spot for so long, never realizing there was an alternative.

Our happiness isn't based on how others treat us; it's based on how we treat others and how we treat ourselves. I had way more control over my own life than I had ever accepted. I had the power to say no to the negativity I gave to myself and others. Guess what? So do you.

So, back to Andrea. She's been pestering me for a while to (in her words) "write a how-to book for the rest of us"—meaning a how-to guide on what it takes to stomp out the negativity that creeps into our everyday interactions. How do we create more joy, less stress, and better relationships? This book is my attempt to teach people how to attain the life they really want to live. Even if no one else reads it, I know Andrea will. Probably.

Since I've now opened my closet and had all the skeletons hop up and do a little dance for you, let me be totally honest about one more thing. I do not consider myself to be a kindness expert. I travel quite a bit for speaking events and interviews, but when people introduce me as a "kindness expert," I cringe. We all get it wrong from time to time. I haven't perfected kindness, but I have experienced the way it can dramatically alter a life, and I know I'm called to share that secret with others.

I see the power of kindness. It's not a fluffy concept that tastes like rainbow-flavored bubblegum. Kindness has real teeth. I know it can change your life, because it changed mine. When I began to be intentional and systematic about kindness, I saw a radical transformation in my life. But don't let the words *intentional* and *systematic* scare you. This is not a weight-loss program or a monthly budget. This is not meant to be one more thing on your to-do list. This is meant to help you see what's happening around you. It's a shift in perspective so you can see the good in the world and join the party. That's when fatigue and emptiness fall away and life becomes fun!

Maybe negativity isn't a problem for you. You've got your inner meanie under control, and anger, resentment, and judgment have no place in your life. Maybe you just feel like something is off.

Like life is just a bit too mundane or predictable or passionless. Perhaps something is missing, but you can't figure out what it is. Good news! Kindness is like the insulating foam that builders use. (At least I think that's what that stuff is. I have never actually built anything.) You spray a little bit of foam and it expands and fills all the empty space. It even helps keep you warm. No matter how kind we are, everybody has something to work on, and kindness can help.

Throughout this book, we're going to identify our own inner meanie. Once we've found him (or her), we're going to crush him by rejecting and replacing our thoughts, by learning from researchers about what's happening in our bodies when we do an act of kindness, and by drawing more positivity into our lives. We'll also deal with the tough stuff, like what to do when people are mean to us, how to react when a good act of kindness goes bad, and how to answer the age-old question, How can I show more kindness to my family and other people who annoy me?

When you latch on to kindness, you have a great tool at your disposal. It calms the places that are judgy and bitter and fills the places in your soul that are empty. All of a sudden, the world is not out to get you. You will realize telemarketers are just people trying to earn a living and the person who waved at you with his middle finger on the freeway is just a guy stuck in a rut of bitterness. The silver lining becomes brighter than the gray clouds and getting out of bed in the morning means looking forward to what the day will bring. Read this book and try it. Be intentional about kindness and look back on your life a year from now. There will be calm in your household, more open conversations with your colleagues, and an immense sense of purpose in your life. Are you longing for those changes? Then tell your inner meanie to hold on tight, because we're about to blow him right out of this popsicle stand.

Lessons from Dinoland

Fargo, North Dakota. It was one of my favorite places to live, but not because of the great accents or the fun phrases I picked up, like "Uff dah," "Oh fer cute!" or "Ya, you betcha."

I loved Fargo for the people. People in Fargo are kind. Well, most of them. A store even came up with the best T-shirts that said "kiND," using the North Dakota abbreviation.

The thing is, nobody's kind all the time. Especially me. Especially when I was thirty-five. Especially when I had a bit too much wine the night before. And it was snowing. And my kids didn't have school. And I felt like I was going to explode if I didn't get my children out of the house so they could expel their excess energy (and loudness).

Are you feeling the not-my-best-day-ever vibes? Ever been there?

I can only imagine the look on my face when I tromped through the food court of our local mall. I had just spent forty-five minutes corralling and loading up three small bodies in -20° temperatures. Now I was inside and sweating, and my kids were whining because they were sweating. I had exhausted any reserves of patience I may have had before leaving the house.

But then we arrived. My sweet oasis: Dinoland.

Dinoland is the place in the mall where parents go when they need to sit and look at their phones while their kids crawl all over gigantic plastic Triceratops and Brontosaurus statues.

My sweet little girl, Jordan, who was seven at the time, ran ahead of me with her five-year-old brother, Charlie. They could not wait to discard their hats and snow boots. Meanwhile, I shuffled behind with a diaper bag of snacks in one arm and my snow-suited toddler, Ben, in the other.

I made it.

Finally, we were all properly unencumbered and situated. Jordan and Charlie stood on top of the T-Rex while Ben sat at my feet digging through the diaper bag for his sippy cup.

There was a young woman sitting next to me with long dark hair. I noticed her because she was wearing real clothes—super cute jeans and little fashionable boots—and she even had her hair combed. I, on the other hand, hadn't made it to the shower that day and was wearing sweatpants. Yes, they were maternity sweatpants. Yes, my youngest child was well past his first birthday. Don't judge; I'm about to do enough of that for the both of us.

I found myself mentally justifying my slovenliness. *It's easy to get up and get ready for the day when you're the babysitter. You don't have a child pulling all of the towels out of your cupboard or being mysteriously quiet in another room. You can take a shower without having to make a decision between shaving your legs or conditioning your hair. Time is of the essence when you're the mom. This girl doesn't know how hard it is. Poor thing, someday she's going to realize what it's like to be a mom. No time for playing "fashionista" then.*

When I looked down, I realized Ben had pulled a Houdini with the snacks and was now helping himself to the Cheerios. On the bright side, he was sharing the ones that fell on the floor with the little boy sitting next to him.

I immediately started to panic under my breath about diseases and dying and possible dog poop that could all be associated with eating off the mall floor.

Dinoland Fashionista, next to me, started giggling. Then she pulled out her (noncontaminated) snacks and handed them to the boy at her feet. He grabbed a handful and then shared with Ben.

It was then I noticed the girl was smiling and doing simple sign language with the toddler. "Please" and "thank you" and "more"—nothing major, but enough to put her in the finals for World's Best Babysitter.

I was trying to figure out how to launch a conversation with her so I could get her phone number without sounding like a stalker or a pathetic loser. If I could get her to babysit my kids, I would have time for naps and other activities that might bring more happiness to my life.

But I didn't have to find the right words, because she did. However, what she said stopped me cold. Fargo cold.

"My son will be a year and a half next week. How old is your son?" Wait. What? *Son? And you showered today?*

This wasn't the World's Best Babysitter. This was the mom. She was maybe seventeen or eighteen, and we had kids the same age.

As we sat side by side watching our kids, who had waddled a short distance away, she lightheartedly shared her story with me, even though it involved an ex-boyfriend and broken promises.

My heart sank as I realized that, even with far fewer resources and a much smaller support system, the Dinoland Fashionista was doing a much better job of being a mom than I was, because I could tell she was *enjoying* it.

This was an unexpected wake-up call.

I don't know when I had stopped enjoying being a mom. Maybe it was after seven straight years without a full night of sleep. Maybe it was after my 728th load of laundry. (By the way, that's a conservative estimate, assuming I'd done two loads of laundry a week for seven years.) I don't know. All I can tell you is this: that day when I walked into the land of dinosaurs, I was drained. Life felt passionless and pointless and mundane—like something everyone else was enjoying and I was only enduring. How could that be when I had the home, husband, and children I had always dreamed of? I knew I was missing something, but I couldn't figure out what that something was. I'd tried to fill that hole with food and alcohol and cigarettes and girls' nights out and shopping, but nothing seemed to stick. I knew I wasn't as happy as the people I saw out in the world and on social media, but I couldn't figure out why.

If you hate me right now, that's okay. I was a bored housewife who had no trouble finding things to complain about. It was affecting my health and the well-being of my family. Looking back, I sort of hate me too. Except if I hadn't been in that place, I wouldn't be writing this book right now. Because of what came next.

Dinoland Fashionista and I started packing up our stuff at about the same time. The little boys needed their afternoon naps.

That was when I got the biggest compliment of my life from a seventeen-year-old mom. "I can tell your kids really love you," she said.

Wow. I so needed to hear that.

Embarrassed by the leaking coming from my eyes, I turned and busied myself with finding a tiny snow boot. That was when a strange voice in my head said, *Stop. Give her some money.* I hadn't heard that voice before, and if it was going to tell me to give away money, I'm not sure I wanted to hear it again.

But I stopped. I reached into my purse and grabbed the last cash in my wallet: two $20 bills.

I turned back to Dinoland Fashionista.

"I need to tell you something," I said.

At this point, her body bristled just a little bit. I think her natural fight-or-flight reaction kicked in, and she braced for me to give her unsolicited advice that would perhaps hurt her feelings. Nevertheless, I continued.

"I know we're never going to see each other again, but I have to tell you something. My best friend died of cancer when we were thirty. That friend taught me about the power of women to lift up other women. I just want to say, I'm glad I met you today. I'm so grateful you would remind me that my kids love me. I forget that sometimes. You have inspired me to be a better mom."

I blabbed on and on for a few more minutes until I realized I was verbally vomiting all over the floor of Dinoland. I stopped talking and handed her the twenties.

She stared at me. Then we both began to cry. Then she threw her arms around me and gave me a big hug.

"Thank you," was all she said.

I'd given her enough money to fill her gas tank and maybe take her kid to McDonald's. What I received in return is hard to put into words. I left the mall and got into my car with a high unlike any other. My skin had goosebumps—and they weren't from the weather. My entire being felt awake, alive, powerful, and, most importantly, purposeful.

In that moment, I knew if other people could feel what I was feeling, they would all want to try it. Kindness would be contagious.

I went home and wrote down everything I was thinking and feeling that day. Then I sent it to the publisher of our local newspaper and asked if I could write a weekly column about kindness. That's the day "Kindness Is Contagious" was born.

I keep waiting to run out of stories of kindness or for the newspaper people to fire me, but so far, neither has happened. In fact, I keep traveling around the country and they keep asking me to keep writing! Yay, kindness!

A young, unsuspecting woman sitting in a mall playland changed the trajectory of my life. Within a year, I was a new person physically (I quit drinking, smoking, and overeating), emotionally (my house became a tantrum-free zone—at least those perpetrated by Mom), and spiritually (I saw my life as having a clear purpose).

But the point here isn't about me and my transformation from kindness. It's about you and the transformation kindness can bring to your life.

I promise you, this is not rocket science. I failed freshman algebra two semesters in a row in college. I couldn't come up with a fancy formula even if I wanted to. This isn't difficult, but it is life changing. And all it takes is going about our lives with a little less attention placed on how we're feeling and a little more attention placed on how others might be feeling.

What does this look like on a daily basis? Let's say we hit the drive-thru first thing in the morning for our cup of joe. We pay, we pull out, and we take our first sip. Instead of getting a mint mocha white chocolate latte with extra whip, we realize we got a double shot dirty chai with coconut milk, no whip. In this moment we have a choice. Will we react in anger or frustration, and let that emotion set the tone for the day, or will we think to ourselves, *Those poor people working in that drive-thru have already been on their feet for four hours. I'm so glad I don't have that job. It must be exhausting.* Maybe we really want the mint drink, so we go back through the line. There we are presented with another choice: *Do I let the employees know that I am not pleased with this delay in my day, or do I speak kindly and remind myself that I make mistakes too?* Since we want people to give us grace, we have to be willing to extend it.

An event planner was setting up a huge three-day conference. She emailed the caterer ahead of time to remind him to have the breakfast buffet hot and ready by 7:00 a.m. Guess what? The caterer didn't show. It was completely his fault. He knew it, but he had made a mistake on his calendar and thought the conference began the following day. He was beside himself. This was a big client. A repeat client. There was nothing he could do except apologize.

I know about this because I was the speaker at the conference. The event planner called me in a panic and said, "We need to move you up in the schedule. You first, then food. Come quickly!"

After I spoke to the group, I spoke to the event planner. "What are you going to do? Are you going to fire the caterer? Give him a piece of your mind?" She said he probably already had a pretty good idea of what was going on in her mind even without her saying anything. But she thought through the situation and realized she really liked that caterer. He had always been great to work with in the past, and she knew losing this account would hurt his business. She decided to give him another chance. The caterer was thrilled and relieved, but the really cool thing was seeing how peaceful the event planner was with her decision. She felt good about giving grace. It was an act of kindness to forgive and move on, and it released her from any feelings of bitterness.

We can't save up our pennies and buy the feelings kindness gives us. We can't make a checklist and decide that once those things are all completed, we will have joy. *When I can afford a bigger house or go on that dream vacation or lose twenty pounds, I will be happy.* These are not the things that will transform our lives. If we truly want to grab on to joy and be free of negativity, we only need to do one thing: wake up each day with the intention of loving others well. Once we do that, we find kindness is sort of like a figure 8. We begin the day thinking we are out to make life better for others, and end the day realizing the one who really benefited was us. We walk down this path and intend to help someone else along the way, but in return we are the ones getting our souls fed. We are the ones whose joy has radically increased.

That freezing cold day in Fargo, back in 2011, I thought I was just paying back the kindness of Dinoland Fashionista. She had made me feel so much better with her compliment, and I'd wanted to do something in return. I had no idea when I handed over the cash that the one whose life would be transformed was mine. I followed that "high" and traced it back to kindness. Kindness was the missing link in my life. When we realize that, when we really take hold of that powerful knowledge and learn how to use it, we become the ones who can help others find their missing link, and the circle of kindness is complete.

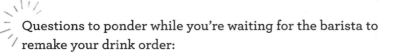

Questions to ponder while you're waiting for the barista to remake your drink order:

1. What is one time when I extended grace to someone who needed it? How did that leave me feeling?
2. What can I do to remind myself each day to pay a little more attention to how other people might be feeling?

Identifying Your Inner Meanie

Are you ready to jump on the kindness train? This is exciting stuff! But first, we need to identify what's holding us back. Let me officially introduce you to your inner meanie. Now, I know what you're thinking. *Hey lady, I don't even know you. What makes you think I have an inner meanie? I'm a very nice person.*

Think you're pretty kind? Okay, let's take a test.

A car pulls out in front of you, forcing you to slam on the brakes. Does your instant reaction have anything to do with raising one of your fingers? Is the word that pops out of your mouth one you'd say in front of your grandma?

How about following the person who is driving 20 in a 35 mph zone? They are making you late. Do you edge up behind them, hoping by hopping on their tail they will realize they need to move faster? Or do you remind yourself of all the reasons why they might be driving so slowly? Maybe it's a new driver feeling anxious and tentative behind the wheel. Maybe it's an old driver who knows their reactions aren't as quick as they once were. Or perhaps the person's mind is so full of worries about what's happening at home they aren't thinking about their speed.

Do you find compassion behind the wheel, or does road rage take a lap around your brain?

Next question: you come home from work and notice the dishwasher needs to be unloaded, the clean laundry needs to be folded, and dinner needs to be on the table before the kids run off to their evening activities. Your spouse walks in the door and immediately plops down on the couch with the remote control.

How do you respond? Do you do the dishes, laundry, and dinner as noisily as possible while stewing about how you're the only one around here who does anything? Or do you take a moment to remind yourself of your spouse's great qualities, then gently ask if they would mind helping out once they've had a chance to relax a bit?

Final question: your boss sends you a short, snippy email that makes no sense and feels ridiculously condescending. Do you hurry over to a coworker who knows exactly what that feels like so the two of you can commiserate together? Or do you think to yourself, *I know nothing about what my boss is going through, but I bet she has some pretty heavy things on her mind right now. I can't control what she says and does, but I can control what I say and do. I refuse to let her toxic juices spread by talking about this with other people in the office*?

Stop for a second and really think about it. When someone makes you mad at work, is the urge to vent nearly overwhelming?

I've been on both sides of every one of those scenarios. It doesn't mean I'm a bad person or a total meanie, it just means I'm a work in progress. So are you.

People tend to see themselves as kind even when the people around them would disagree. Fellow kindness warrior Barbara Hirsh did a survey for her book, *Live Kinder*.[1] She asked eighty juveniles expelled from public schools if they thought of themselves as kind. More than half of those kids were affiliated with a gang. Every single one of them said they were kind. When she asked why they felt that way, they pointed to individual acts of kindness they had done, like helping their mom carry groceries into the house.

We might look at our individual acts, like carrying in groceries or letting someone in line in front of us and think, *Sure, I'm kind*, but the kindness I'm talking about goes much deeper. It's about how we see people and situations. It's not about doing; it's about *being*. We can do an act of kindness, but it's not until we are being vessels of kindness in our thoughts, words, and deeds that we see radical life change. The reason we need to get a realistic grip on our kindness level is because our kindness isn't about other people; it's about us.

Take those questions you just answered. The first scenario deals with complete strangers, the people in traffic you'll never see again. The second scenario deals with your family, the people who often get to see you at your worst. The third scenario deals with your coworkers, the people you go on vacation to escape.

What's the one common denominator in each situation?

You.

Kindness isn't about them; it's about you. That's the big secret behind this whole kindness mind shift. We can change jobs and divorce our spouse and hide in a cave, but we'll still be with ourselves. There is no escaping. If we allow ourselves to get caught up in a tornado of emotions, eventually something will wreck our perfectly formed bubble, and we'll be back to blaming and complaining and stomping our feet.

So, what's the solution? We've got to take our thoughts captive. We have to tell them who's boss, and keep telling them, until they begin to naturally lean in the direction of compassion all by themselves.

Is that even possible? Yep. Your brain is creating new path-ways every day. You teach your mind how to react in future situations by how you react in the current ones.

For example, anyone walking into my mudroom would assume I either have twenty-four children or that each of my kids has eight feet. That's how many shoes I get to trip over every time I walk into the house. My natural inclination might be to yell something like, "Kids! Get in here and put your shoes away *now*! And no, you cannot finish your video game first! By the way, you're all grounded from electronics for the rest of your lives."

I'm not saying I've actually said any of those words . . . it's purely hypothetical. Sort of.

Instead of allowing my mind and my mouth to create that sort of environment in our household, I work hard to try a different approach.

I look at the pink crocs and give thanks for the teenage boy who has been proud to wear pink ever since 2015, when his momma was diagnosed with breast cancer.

I look at the stinky running shoes and give thanks for the teenage daughter who made the varsity cross country team as a freshman.

I look at the littlest shoes and give thanks for a completely healthy elementary school boy who was born with a heart murmur.

I still ask them to pick up their shoes, but it's done with respect, which is exactly how I want them to learn to speak to people both inside and outside our home.

Step 1: Think about What You're Thinking About

The key to kindness is to stop worrying about what other people are saying and doing and how their behavior is affecting us.

Remember, this isn't about other people. It's about us and what's going on in our heads that is causing us to see red the moment something bugs us. Instead of thinking about others, we take the first step toward living an authentically kind life by thinking about what we're thinking about.

So that's Step 1. Easy peasy. Start thinking about what you're thinking about. Take a moment throughout the day to ask yourself, *What am I thinking about right now?*

Let's do it together at this very moment. What are you thinking about? Hopefully you're thinking about the words you're reading on this page, so maybe let's rewind to a bit earlier in the day. What were you thinking about before you picked up this book? Let me guess:

- Where you have to be next.
- What time you need to pick up a child.
- What you need to get from the grocery store.
- If your child will ever become potty-trained.
- If the new boss at work is going to like you as much as the old boss did.
- If we all are going to get cancer from talking on our cell phones while pumping gas.
- Why that lady in aisle three has so many bottles of wine in her cart.
- Why teenage girls wear such short dresses these days.
- How those people should really do a better job of disciplining their children.

It seems that most people have thoughts that fall into one of three categories: hurry, worry, or jury. "Hurry" includes those thoughts about our to-do lists. It's the frantic *Where I need to be and what I need to be doing* thoughts. If you live on this planet,

I'm certain at one time or another you have been hustled around by our friend hurry.

"Worry" is what happens when we let our minds wander. We may think we're just walking through hypothetical situations, but in fact our anxiety increases and our love for other people decreases just by allowing our brain to park in the land of what-if. *What if my husband cheats on me? What if my son's heart is broken by that girl?*

Let's face it, there's not a single thing we can do about those things we're worrying about, so why borrow trouble from tomorrow? The problem is, usually we don't even notice we're worrying about something until after it has shifted our mood and ruined a good chunk of our day.

The third category, "jury," used to be my go-to hangout. Being in charge of everyone else's actions is exhausting, but my inner meanie excelled at being both judge and jury for myself and everyone around me. If I ate too many cookies after dinner, I declared myself a hopeless sugar addict. If someone else's kids ate too many cookies after dinner, I declared them children with poor parenting. Do you ever find yourself doing that? Picking on yourself or others just because that's where the sharpest dart landed in your mind?

Here's a revelation: you don't have to dwell on every thought that pops into your brain. Don't believe me? Let me take you on a little trip. Let's see . . . I'm in the mood for a quiet beach. Ready? There you are, eyes closed, completely relaxed on a deserted, soft, sandy, beach. You can feel the warmth of the sun as it radiates against your face. The gentle caress of the ocean breeze ebbs and flows across your skin in time with the rhythm of the waves. The smell of sunscreen wafts through the air, reminding you of your carefree teenage summers.

Can you feel yourself immersed in that moment? It's beautiful and relaxing, and you want to stay there forever. Breathe in that favorite vacation memory and savor it. You deserve this moment by yourself.

Now think of the top five things you buy every time you go to the grocery store. For me it's milk, bread, bananas, Cheerios, and Froot Loops. Are you still sitting oceanside on your sandy beach? No, you're in the dairy aisle of Pick-n-Save.

We have the ability to control our thoughts, but first we have to recognize what we're thinking.

Again, back to Step 1. Think about what you're thinking about. Check in with yourself in the shower, on the drive to work, and while you're making dinner. Are you in the zone of hurry, worry, or jury? If so, it's time to move on to Step 2.

Step 2: Reject and Replace

When I first started to examine my thoughts, I didn't like what I found. My mind was sort of a scary place to be, all dark and chaotic and filled with freaky creatures jumping up out of nowhere. Sure, every once in a while, a unicorn or some cotton candy would float through, but normally my brain was a road map for the best Halloween fright-night corn maze ever. Yuck.

Thoughts hold immense power over our lives. I knew I was guilty of letting my mind wander around unaccompanied, and I could see the way my thoughts were playing into my actions and setting the tone for my day. I began thinking about what I was thinking about, and when I noticed my mind veering to an unhealthy place, I started intentionally rejecting and replacing the thought.

Every time I realized I was thinking something a meanie would think, I said to myself, *I reject that thought.*

(Friend, let me pause and say when I started this gig I had to say *I reject that thought* hundreds of times a day. Literally.)

There I was in the gym, looking at my fat stomach in the gigantic mirror, when it would dawn on me that I was judging myself too harshly. *I reject that thought.* Or driving in super slow traffic and wishing the person who got into the accident would have been considerate enough to pull off to the side of the road first. *I reject that thought.* Or walking into the living room and wondering if being single would be a better alternative to seeing my husband's socks on the living room floor for the third night in a row. *I reject that thought.*

You catch my drift.

I got really good at telling myself *I reject that thought,* but since that's not enough to move our minds from one spot to the next, I also had to replace the negative thought. For months I carried around a tiny piece of paper in my pocket. Nine words in blue ink on a white background said, "Love, joy, peace, patience, kindness, goodness, faithfulness, gentleness, and self-control" (Gal. 5:22–23).

For me, these words from the book of Galatians were things I wanted more of in my life. I wanted to grow in each of those areas—but first I had to *remember* them. I'm not so good at memorizing. which turned out to be a benefit in this case. After I would think the words, *I reject that thought,* I would force my brain to recite that list of nine words. *Love, joy, peace . . .* for a long time I could get three or four words out but then would inevitably forget what came next and have to pull out my little piece of paper. Once I finally got them all memorized, I then found something new to carry around to force my mind to continue to search for positive thoughts to replace the negative. My new piece of paper said, "Fix your thoughts on what is true, and honorable, and right, and pure, and lovely, and admirable. Think about things that are excellent and worthy of praise" (Phil. 4:8).

My words came from the Bible, because that's an important book to me, but if that doesn't resonate with you, go online and find a quote or mantra or list of words that matter to you and then write them down and stick them in your pocket. The next time you catch yourself thinking thoughts that wind you up or drag you down, pull out that paper and start memorizing.

You'll be surprised by how quickly you can retrain your brain.

Questions to ponder while you're standing in line at the grocery store (instead of reading the magazine headlines about the lady who gave birth to an alien):

1. What do you find yourself thinking about in each category?

   • Hurry:

   • Worry:

   • Jury:

2. What words will you work on memorizing to replace the meanie's thoughts?

   I reject that thought and (put new thought here). Make it something difficult enough to force you to stop and think about it so you can move your brain away from the old thought.

What Actual Experts Are Saying about Kindness

Although I'm not a researcher, I am a geek for kindness research. Thankfully, the real experts have a lot to say about what kindness does to our minds and our bodies. There truly are chemical reactions happening in our bodies in response to kindness. It's nice to know I'm not just making this all up.

The first time I was asked to speak about kindness in front of an audience was in 2012. I had been writing the "Kindness Is Contagious" column for about a year, and apparently that convinced people I was enough of an expert to speak on the subject. Knowing I really didn't know what I was talking about, I turned to my trusty laptop to find the latest findings on kindness. You know what I found? Nothing. Sir Google, who can find 1,780,000 results in 0.50 seconds for "proper toilet posture," couldn't find a thing about the scientific evidence of kindness.

But after a little more digging, I came across a man named Allan Luks. He was the pioneer of kindness research, only he didn't call it kindness. His book, published in 1992, was titled *The Healing Power of Doing Good*. Allan is an expert in the fields of volunteerism, mentorship, and social change, stemming from his work in the 1990s as executive director of Big Brothers Big Sisters of New York City. It was during that time that Allan realized some of the volunteers were experiencing what he coined the "helper's high." It's the physical feeling people experience when helping others, sort of like a runner's high only without the sweat.

Allan surveyed more than three thousand volunteers, both men and women, to figure out which variables caused people to experience the helper's high and what physical benefits they were actually receiving. He concluded that helpers are ten times more likely to be in good health than those who don't volunteer.

As he explained in the book, and then again in person when I interviewed him for my weekly show, *The Kindness Podcast*, three things are essential to attaining the helper's high.

First, the helping has to be consistent. That doesn't mean you are repeating the same act of kindness over and over; it means you are consistently looking for and acting on ways to help others. It has to happen on a regular basis. I've definitely experienced the helper's high from a one-time interaction with another person, but being intentional and consistent about kindness creates new pathways in the brain that get you back to that helper's high again and again. Buying coffee for the same person every morning is probably going to get boring. Finding one new person to interact with each day will keep you alert to the needs of the people around you.

Second, the helping has to include strangers or people we don't know very well. As I'll explain more in a minute, stepping out of our comfort zones is scary, and that elicits a quick release of endorphins, the fight-or-flight hormone. I have to say, I feel good when I help a neighbor or a friend, but I feel great when I do something for a total stranger.

Before we move on to the third essential element to gaining that helper's high, let's take a little pop quiz.

Which act of kindness releases the most chemicals into your body?

1. Writing a check to a homeless shelter.
2. Cooking a meal for a homeless shelter.
3. Serving a meal at a homeless shelter.
4. They are all equal.

Did you guess? No peeking at the answer in the next paragraph. Ah, I see you wanting to peek!

Okay, I'll let you down from your suspense. The correct answer is number 3: serving a meal at a homeless shelter.

Don't get me wrong; writing a check and financially supporting nonprofit organizations is essential. They'd all go under if it wasn't for people like you and me who have a heart to give. That's certainly an important element of helping.

Cooking a meal for a homeless shelter is also important. So is any behind-the-scenes work you do to make life more comfortable for other people. Those ladies in the church kitchen who prepare an entire buffet of deviled eggs, seven-layer salad, and snickerdoodles so that people are rewarded with food after sitting through my message of kindness are so very kind. That type of kindness matters, but I think what Allan Luks is saying is that sometimes we have to step out of the kitchen.

That's where the third and final step to achieving a helper's high comes in. Here it is: personal contact. Sitting down and having a conversation with someone different from us is life-changing. We learn that our way may not be the only way. We build compassion, which shuts down the voice of our inner meanie, and we cultivate gratitude in our hearts.

I'm a big fan of homeless people, or perhaps I should use the more politically correct term, people without a home. Now, I'm not saying, "Yay! Homelessness is awesome! We should all try it!" I've never been homeless. I have no idea how that feels. People who sit on a piece of cardboard for hours at a time have nothing in common with me. Or so it might seem.

When I say I'm a fan, I mean I love to talk to homeless people. Their stories are fascinating. I always learn something new, and I always walk away feeling like I saw someone who might be invisible to others, and he or she saw me too. And I always leave feeling more grateful than when I arrived.

A few years ago my family traveled to Disney World. We ventured off-site on a rainy afternoon to check out a restaurant. My husband ushered our three kids to the restaurant door while I ran next door to a Walgreens. As I walked out of the store, I noticed a man sitting under the awning with his back against the brick wall. He wasn't asking for money. He was just sitting there, and it looked like he might have been sitting there for a while.

I rushed past him and headed into the restaurant. As I sat down at the table, my very intuitive husband said, "What?"

I explained about the man outside, and my husband rolled his eyes in a joking way and said, "Go."

I crossed the parking lot in the rain and approached the man. I could see he was doing a crossword puzzle. I knelt down and said, "Need any help with six across? I'm pretty good at crosswords. Hi, I'm Nicole."

He smiled at me and said, "I'm Steve."

"Well, Steve," I continued, "my family is next door having dinner, and I wondered if maybe you were hungry. I'd love to buy you a burger."

"Oh, no. I couldn't. I'm fine. Thanks so much." His response was quick and slightly embarrassed.

I didn't want to leave him on that note, so I started asking him where he was from (Illinois), how he got to Florida (he had a son), and what interested him (airplanes).

Then I said again, "Are you sure you wouldn't like something to eat?"

This time, as a friend, he accepted. "A burger sure does sound good."

I went back to the restaurant and ordered Steve's meal. My kids were ages twelve, ten, and six at the time. When the server brought out the to-go bag, it was my ten-year-old son, Charlie, who asked if he could help deliver it.

We walked outside together, and I introduced Charlie to Steve. We talked a bit about airplanes and Illinois, and after a few minutes, Charlie and I met the rest of our family at the car so we could continue our grand Disney adventure. Still under the awning, Steve set down his crossword and picked up his burger.

I love Disney, but the pixie dust I found on that vacation wasn't in the park. It was on the sidewalk next to a Walgreens. In a five-minute conversation, Steve reminded me to forget about the long lines and the tired feet and the price of admission and focus on the real magic of the moment.

I had a helper's high that lasted the rest of the vacation and beyond, and it only cost me eight bucks.

Have you ever had that feeling? Maybe you're flying out to relax on the beach and yet are totally annoyed you have to sit in a middle seat on the airplane. Then you see someone exchange their first-class seat with a person in military fatigues. All of a sudden your situation isn't of interest to you. It's not worth complaining about because you realize (1) how good you've got it, and (2) there are some pretty great people in this world.

When I was talking to Steve, I didn't intend to change my day. I was on vacation after all, so my day was going well. I was relaxed and happy. But thanks to a short interaction that was just outside my comfort zone, deep inside my body a major explosion of feel-good chemicals was happening.

The more I study kindness, the more fascinating it becomes. There's more to it than just rerouting a bad day. When it comes to our health, engaging in acts of kindness ranks right up there with exercise and healthy eating!

If I told you I could take away physical pain in your body, reduce your anxiety, sprinkle your life with more happiness, or lower your blood pressure, which would you choose? Would you agree that at least one of those things sounds appealing?

The good news is, you don't have to choose. Kindness releases four feel-good chemicals that do all those things.

Endorphins are the body's natural painkiller. They kick in when you physically exert yourself or when your body thinks it might need to protect itself. When you talk to a stranger or put yourself out there a little during an act of kindness, your body is confused about whether or not it needs to be on guard. It releases endorphins in preparation for fight or flight, giving you a boost of strength and energy in case quick action is needed. When I talked to Steve, I got an immediate jolt of energy that was equivalent to the best power nap ever.

Serotonin is your body's antidepressant. Stress increases your cortisol (the stress hormone) and decreases your serotonin. That is the opposite of how your body best functions. Perpetually kind people have 23 percent less cortisol running through their bodies. They even age slower than the average population. Who needs a fountain of youth when you have kindness on your side?

Serotonin is also the body's natural antianxiety medication. University of British Columbia researchers found that people with high levels of anxiety had a significant improvement in mood after doing kind acts for others at least six times a week (basically making it part of their daily routine). This is important to me, personally, because I've had to deal with anxiety as one of the side effects of my breast cancer medication. Although I'm now healthy and cancer-free, I'll be on the "no-more-cancer" pill (Tamoxifen) for several more years. On the days when I wake up feeling especially agitated, I know I need to get my eyes off myself and help another person.

Another interesting trait of serotonin is that it's easy to fool. Serotonin doesn't know the difference between real and imaginary. The hormone is released into your body during the act of kindness, but when you lie in bed later that night and mentally replay the act of kindness, serotonin is released once again.

This is the reason why gratitude journals are so effective at brightening our mood. When we take time to recall in detail the goodness in our lives, serotonin starts kicking in and releasing those feel-good vibes.

Dopamine is that wonderful feeling of being rewarded. This falls in line with the concept of "retail therapy." You go buy something you don't need because it feels good to be rewarded for having a hard day. It's also the reason I have a special section of my freezer for pints of Ben & Jerry's. I like the feeling of being rewarded, and dopamine makes that happen.

Kindness lights up the brain's pleasure center, sending dopamine coursing through your body and making you feel like you were actually the recipient of an act of kindness instead of the giver.

The final feel-good chemical released during kindness is *oxytocin*. Oxytocin has both psychological and physical effects on the body. According to Dr. David Hamilton, acts of kindness create an emotional warmth, sort of like when you cuddle, which is why oxytocin is known as the cuddle hormone.

Want to live longer? Kindness is considered cardio-protective because it releases oxytocin, which produces *nitric oxide* that widens the blood vessels, in turn reducing blood pressure. Yep, you heard me right. Kindness can lower your blood pressure. In a study of volunteers over age fifty-five, kindness is proven to protect against heart disease and literally lengthen participants' life spans even more than exercise! That's all thanks to oxytocin.

Christine Carter, author of *Raising Happiness: Ten Simple Steps for More Joyful Kids and Happier Parents*, says,

> People who volunteer tend to experience fewer aches and pains. Giving help to others protects overall health twice as much as aspirin protects against heart disease. People 55 and older who volunteer for two or more organizations have an impressive 44% lower likelihood of dying early, and that's after sifting out every other contributing factor, including physical health, exercise, gender, habits like smoking, marital status and many more. This is a stronger effect than exercising four times a week or going to church.[1]

It's not just our health that benefits from kindness, though. Amazingly, it can also increase both our wealth and our happiness. Let me explain.

You'd think giving away your money would lead to having no money, right? Wrong.

It pays to be kind! A professor at the University of California-Berkeley says people who are compassionate and in tune with other people's emotions are more successful at work. People trust you more and have better interactions with you, which often means a payoff when you ask your boss for a raise.

Kindness can also jump-start a cascade of positive social consequences. Helping others leads people to like you, appreciate you, and reciprocate in your time of need.

My entire family saw this particular benefit in our own lives in an immense way when I was diagnosed with breast cancer in 2015. We had moved to a new town the year before, which turned out to be just enough time to make some really great friends and spread the word that our family loved kindness. As soon as the diagnosis came through, cards, gifts, and well-wishes came pouring in from people in both Fargo, North Dakota (our former home), and Athens, Ohio (our new home). My daughter, Jordan, decided to raise money for other women with breast cancer by sewing coffee cup sleeves and asking for a five-dollar donation. She raised $5,741 in three months thanks to those same friends, who shared her story on social media. Jordan was eleven at the time.

Eventually, Walmart got wind of her mission and bought 207,000 of her "Cozys for the Cure" products. Within three years, Jordan had raised more than $100,000 for the Susan G. Komen foundation. Today you can find people using "Cozys" in New York, California, Texas, Florida, Colorado, Wisconsin, and a whole lot of other states. I'd call that a pretty significant cascade of positive social consequences for a girl who was just trying to help others and for a mom with a little newspaper column on kindness.

Harvard Business School has also done a pretty amazing job of showing it feels better to give than to receive. The school's research of data from 136 countries shows people who are financially generous are happier than those who keep a tight fist on their wallets. The feelings of emotional well-being crossed cultural contexts and were consistent in countries where people had a little to give versus a lot.

Speaking of happiness, researchers believe practicing random acts of kindness makes you feel happier because you begin to think more highly of yourself. You begin to see your own power and ability to make the world a better place. People who are kind focus more on positive social interactions. Instead of dwelling on the bad things that happen throughout the day, those who are kind begin magnifying and remembering the good.

Who would you assume benefits the most from an act of kindness? Maybe before this little science lesson you would have said, "The receiver of the kindness benefits the most." Perhaps, after hearing about the chemical reactions taking place in our bodies, you'd say, "The giver definitely has the greatest reward."

What if I were to tell you that kindness works as a trifecta? According to Brooke Jones of the Random Acts of Kindness Foundation, the chemical effects of kindness are felt by the giver, the receiver—and all the witnesses.

Let's say you're waiting in the checkout lane at the grocery store. You decide to reach forward and pay for the groceries of the person in front of you. You have instantly changed your day and the day of the person who just scored free groceries. But you have also changed the day of the checkout clerk, the person standing behind you, and the person bagging the groceries. Each of them is on high alert because something out of the ordinary is happening, which is then replaced by a sense of well-being as they spend the rest of their shift thinking about the goodness of people.

This idea of kindness working as a trifecta, with the giver, receiver, and witnesses all benefiting, is also why it is essential to pay attention to what we're feeding our minds.

Two people find themselves scrolling through posts on social media. One eventually stands up and heads out with a skip in her step to go pick up her kids. The other one sinks deeper and deeper into her swivel chair, dreading whatever else is on the docket for the day.

What's the difference?

Is it that one is picking up kids and the other is at the office? Nope.

Is it that one was on Facebook and the other was on Instagram? Nope.

Is it that one is looking forward to going on vacation and the other just got back? Nope.

Have you figured it out?

It comes down to what they were looking at on social media. Are we allowing our brains to focus on the divisive political comments and the bragging neighbor's latest, greatest vacation? If we fill our feeds with things that ignite our hungry egos or put us in the position of judge and jury, you can bet we are going to feel depleted. From that perspective, the world looks big and overwhelming and mean. Everybody else looks like they've got it together, and our own meager lives can never compete. We're left staring at a screen wishing things were different.

On the other hand, when we set up our news feeds to include pictures of cute puppies and inspiring quotes and fun-loving stories of kindness, we can restore our faith in humanity and preserve or even increase the energy we take into the day.

I was eavesdropping on a conversation between thirteen-year-old boys the other day. They were talking about who they follow on Instagram. Once they got past all the celebrity athletes, they mentioned a name I hadn't heard before. Peaceful Barb. I thought they were making fun of her, so I chimed in to ask about her posts.

"She's awesome! She's always saying things to make you feel good."

The boys weren't kidding. Peaceful Barb is constantly reminding people they are good enough and that it's all going to be okay.

People often say to me, "There's just so much bad in the world." We begin to look around and believe there is indeed more bad in the world than good. But that's simply not true. The negative stuff is just louder. Televisions and newspapers and computers shout out all the terrible things happening in our world because, thanks to human nature, we all turn to look at the train wreck. We forget the train wreck isn't the only thing happening.

I worked as a news reporter and television anchor for about a decade. I also produced evening newscasts. I can tell you that we in the news biz look for twenty-nine minutes of shocking, breaking news and then one minute of something sweet to put at the end of the show. Television people are in the business of giving people what they want, and what they want is to be in the know. Viewers want something that is sensational and entertaining, or they want information that will help them protect themselves and their families from potential harm. News outlets are not in the business of making sure we also know of the expansive good deeds happening around the world, because they simply don't sell.

In 2014, a Russian news website reported only good news for one whole day. It lost two-thirds of its readers. The next day it went back to hard (bad) news. Its readership returned, ready to see the next train wreck.[2]

So, how do we stay informed and positive at the same time? When Mr. Rogers was a little boy and scary things would happen, his wise mother would tell him, "Look for the helpers."[3] Surrounding the negativity is a team of people working to clean up the mess. They are lending their kindness to situations that need goodness breathed into them. I have yet to see something terrible happen that hasn't been immediately followed by something breathtakingly beautiful. Take the 9/11 attacks. Following the terrible photos of people jumping out of buildings came story after story of people who showed up to help. Or consider California wildfires. At the same time people are sorting through the wreckage of their lives, others are donating hard-earned dollars or flying in to lend a hand.

Big acts of kindness or little—it doesn't really matter. They are happening, and I believe they far outnumber the negative, but we have to be willing to look for them. That means paying close attention to the type of information we are allowing into our brains and setting ourselves up for success by "booby-trapping" our days with reminders of the good happening around us.

We can set up those traps by subscribing to daily morning emails of kindness. I love the Good News Network[4] and also

Morning Smile by Inspire More.[5] We can fill our minds with good stuff by filling our social media feeds with good stuff, like people spreading messages of hope and positivity. My kids introduced me to Peaceful Barb on Instagram, and it's amazing how she can cross all generations with her messages.[6] Also, reading books before bed that include stories of people helping people will calm our bodies and get those gentle feelings of well-being flowing as we drift off to sleep. (I heard of a really good book called *Kindness Is Courageous: 100 Stories to Remind You People Are Brave and Kind.* It's by a talented writer named Nicole Phillips.)

We're going to watch the news and look at our phones throughout the day. That's a given. We get to decide whether we are going to be the person who feels energized by doing so or the one who is left drained and defeated.

Questions to ponder when your spouse's snoring keeps you up at night:

1. What self-soothing actions, like a "retail therapy" shopping spree or eating pints of ice cream, do I currently use during a hard day to ignite the feel-good hormones in my body?

2. What sources can I use to add more positivity into my television, reading, and social media outlets?

Drawing More Kindness into Your Life

Saying Yes to the Positive

My husband, the college basketball coach, travels a lot for work. He goes from city to city, game to game, spending at least one night in a hotel room for each trip. I stay home with the kids until tournament time comes. Then we all hit the road together.

You might think I pack up the household and follow the coach because I am a supportive wife who enjoys cheering on her husband. Nope. I'm in it for the perks. You see, when my husband is coaching in a tournament, he doesn't get just any old ordinary room. Most of the time, he gets one of the best rooms the hotel has to offer. Think posh multiroom suites overlooking the city lights, far away from the noisy elevators.

My husband walks into the room, throws his stuff on a chair, and gets to work. I wander around the vast expanse of our mini-mansion, feeling the thread count of the sheets, taking pictures of the view, and checking out the brand name on the tiny shampoo and conditioner bottles.

I get especially delighted when I walk into the room and find (tah-dah!) a welcome gift basket. It usually includes something both sweet and salty from the local area and a small memento from the tournament sponsor.

I am a sucker for a gift basket. If I ever become a Hollywood celebrity, I already know my favorite part will be the swag bags they hand out at the fancy awards shows.

It's not that I especially love free stuff; I just love it when people are kind to me. Like really love it. I get such a kick out of preferred treatment it's almost disturbing. But come on, don't you love it too?

Knowing that someone thought of me and took the time to put together something that would make me feel special is just the best. My kids roll their eyes as I point to the gift basket and sing out, "Kindness!"

You might think my love language is giving and receiving gifts. It's not. I prefer acts of service. To me, the person picking out the gift was actually doing an act of service, just like the hotel staff who neatly placed the little bottle of lotion on the bathroom sink.

I'm spoiled when I go to these yearly basketball tournaments, but I'm also spoiled at home. I find people constantly doing and saying nice things while I'm at the drive-thru window, sitting down at a restaurant, going to a movie, and at the doctor's office. At the very least, people engage me with a smile that makes me feel seen and appreciated. Why? Because I leave behind the negativity and walk into a room expecting people to be kind. Therefore, I make eye contact and smile and say nice things to them. When we look for the good in others, we will find it. Our brains zero in on the positivity. If we're looking for the negative, though, that's what we'll find instead.

Part of being on a kindness adventure is learning how to call more of it into our lives. Sometimes I want to do something kind for another person "just because," but often it stems out of the great appreciation I have for how people have treated me.

So how do we attract more kindness into our lives? Let's look at six ways.

1. Expect People to Be Kind

How often do you enter a room and consciously think to yourself, *People in this office are going to be kind to me?* If anything, we're usually filled with dismay about having to run a particular errand, or we allow our inner meanie to remind us the last time we talked with the receptionist she was a little snippy.

I have two friends who go to the post office several times a week for their businesses. One actually stopped going and started sending her husband because she couldn't stand the treatment she got from the clerks. She became acutely aware of what she perceived as an employee attitude problem, and she couldn't enter the building without instantly feeling a sense of negativity.

When I found out another friend also goes to that same post office, I asked her what she thought of the staff. "Oh!" she exclaimed, "I love them! Dan and Darcy and Jerry all take such great care of me. They're always so friendly."

Wait, what?

These are the same people my first friend was dealing with, but with a totally different outcome.

Here's what I think could've happened. Friend #1 went into the post office one day, and the clerk she was working with had something heavy on his mind and therefore didn't smile. He came across as abrupt and rude. Maybe the next time my friend went in she got a different employee who was starving and in a rush because she was minutes away from her lunch break. The third time, perhaps my friend had something mislabeled and was asked to go to the back of the line because it was a busy time of the day.

The negativity overwhelms her. She feels like no one likes her, they are all picking on her, and everyone around her is a little bit mean. Now that's the opinion she takes with her every time she goes back to the post office. Even good interactions are tainted by previous negative experiences.

On the flip side, friend #2 walked in expecting people to be nice to her. When the man at the counter was distracted, she slowed down enough to recognize his behavior had nothing to do with her. She thanked him sincerely and wished him a good day. When she got in line with the woman who was feeling hungry and rushed, she made simple conversation and found out the woman had skipped breakfast that day. My friend jokingly says that means there will be calories left for ice cream tonight. When she's asked to go to the back of the line for the mislabeled package, my friend looks behind her at all the other people waiting and realizes these poor clerks are going to be on their feet for a long time today. "My bad!" she says with a wink as she steps to the side.

We have a choice to see the world through the lens of kindness. It doesn't mean people are actually being kind; it just means we are expecting them to be kind, so when they aren't we figure they must have a good reason. It helps us shake off anything that might mildly offend us and build compassion toward the other person.

2. Look for the Silver Lining in Every Situation

We can draw more kindness into our lives by forcing our brains to process everything through the filter that asks, *What positive will come from this situation?*

Remember that old movie *Pollyanna*? It starred Hayley Mills back in the 1960s and was based on a book written in 1913 about an excessively optimistic child. The little girl, an orphan, plays "The Glad Game," in which she encourages others around her to find something to be glad about in every situation. She's living with her cranky spinster aunt who only takes her in under a sense of obligation. Apparently everyone else in the little Vermont town is crabby too, because it's a shock to their systems when Pollyanna teaches them to look for the good around them.

Spoiler alert: stop reading if you're going to watch the movie. Or read this and then watch the movie anyway. It's totally worth two hours and fourteen minutes of your time.

At the conclusion of the movie, Pollyanna has something really bad happen to her (as if having both of her parents die wasn't enough), and she loses all hope. Negativity is knocking at the door. That's when the townspeople sweep in to love on that child something fierce and remind her of her own game, which has taught them so much about creating joy and changed their outlook on life.

The term *Pollyanna* is sometimes used to describe someone who is annoyingly positive. As in, "She has no grip on reality; she's such a Pollyanna."

But I think those people need to watch the movie. Or read the book.

The point of looking for the silver lining is not so we can ignore the bad stuff. It's so the bad stuff doesn't take more than its fair share of attention in our brains. We aren't hiding our heads in the sand; we are using the negativity remedy by standing tall and saying, "There is more to this situation than first meets the eye."

Let's say the electricity is turned off in your house because you didn't have money to pay the bill. Instead of sitting in the dark feeling like an awful parent, you can remind yourself that lessons about budgeting are painful, but they are an important part of teaching your kids to survive in this world.

Maybe you get into a car wreck and have to rely on a coworker to pick you up for a few weeks. That doesn't mean the sky is falling; it means you get some time to know another person a little better.

When I was diagnosed with breast cancer, everyone outside our household felt sorry for us. But everyone inside our household cherished the way we began to spend more time together. We spoke a little sweeter and listened more intently.

There is a story I love about a college professor who taught his students a very valuable lesson. As they all sat in a large assembly hall waiting for the lecture, the professor instead showed them a white piece of paper with a black dot in the middle. He asked them to take a few minutes and write about what they saw.

He collected the papers a bit later and, right there in class, began reading the answers the students had written. Some saw the black dot as an ink stain. Some saw it as a hole into another existence. A few commented on whether it was really black or maybe just dark blue pretending to be black.

The one commonality was that every student wrote about the black dot. Not a single person wrote about the white space.

It's often like that in our lives. We focus so much on the financial trouble, the hurt feelings, the cancer diagnosis, that we forget the rest of our lives is filled with white space, the place where creativity and love and kindness live.

The more we look at the black dots in our lives, the larger they become, until we have difficulty shifting our eyes to anything else. But the reverse is also true: the more we focus on the white space, the smaller those black dots become, until they really don't attract much of our attention. We'll always know they are there. We aren't hiding from them. We just aren't allowing them to overtake the page.

So go ahead, be a Pollyanna. Look for the silver lining in every situation. If you truly can't find anything positive about your circumstances, then focus on this: someday you will be able to use this experience to help another person. Knowing that is sure to add white space to your life.

3. Verbalize Your Gratitude

There is a debate happening over whether or not people should say "Thank you." (Please excuse me while I roll my eyes. Do we truly have nothing better to think about? Sorry. That was my inner meanie escaping.)

In one camp are the people who say the words have lost their meaning. They are thrown around so often it's like hearing someone cough. There is also the dilemma of someone's duty to you versus their willingness to go above and beyond to help you.

I suppose when we go to a restaurant and the waiter refills our water, we are not obligated to say thank you. At some of those fancy restaurants, there is a person whose entire job is to refill the water glasses. You take a sip and there he is, ready to top you off. So yes, perhaps we don't need to continually repeat the phrase.

But what about when your boss asks you to do a report and have it on her desk by 5:00? You walk into her office and hand her the report. She mumbles, "Yeah, okay," and you turn around and walk away. Or maybe she looks you in the eye and says, "Thank you. This will be a big help for our meeting tomorrow." Which response leaves you more willing to assist in the future?

Several studies show that expressing gratitude can create people who are invested in seeing you succeed. One study in particular wanted to see if gratitude had an effect on the person being thanked, like motivation to be kind in the future.

Sixty-nine people were asked to provide feedback on a cover letter written by a fake student named Eric. Eric emailed the participants to let them know he received their feedback and then turned around and asked them for help again. With just a general acknowledgment of receipt from Eric, 32 percent agreed to help him again. When Eric added a personal note of thanks, the number of people willing to give more of their time shot up to 66 percent.

In a similar study, seventy college students were asked to give feedback on high school students' college application essays. A week later, the college students each received a note from their high school student saying they'd received their edits. But half also included a personal note expressing their gratitude.

The college students were then given a questionnaire asking their perception of the student and whether they would be willing to provide contact information so they could connect with the high schooler in the future. Those who received a thank-you note rated their student mentee in a more favorable light and were more willing to give their contact info for future interaction.

Here's one more nonscience example you may have experienced in your own life.

You know those parties they throw in elementary school classrooms the day before kids are let out for winter break? Parents are asked to pitch in with a fruit tray and pretzels or maybe cute holiday napkins? Let's say you decide to go all out and make tiny edible snowmen out of marshmallows and chocolate chips. It takes you six hours to put them together, but you saw them on Pinterest and they just looked so cute and, well, you know, it sort of seemed worth it to spend the night in the kitchen.

You pour a strong cup of coffee and head into the school with your delightful treats. You gingerly set them on the counter in the office and then go home for a nap.

Your child gets off the bus and the first thing you say is, "How did everyone like the snowmen?" Your son replies with a long story about how someone dropped pretzels on the floor and everyone ate them, completely ignoring your need to be acknowledged as World's Best Room Parent. You realize your son is oblivious, so you wait for the email from the teacher telling you to start your own cooking show. It never comes. You figure the card is in the mail. It's not.

You didn't create marshmallow snowmen because you wanted to be acknowledged, but a "Hey, thanks! Those were really a hit!" would have gone far. I don't know about you, but if it's me, the next time the treat sign-up sheet goes around, I might just settle for sending in a box of Fruit Roll-Ups.

Okay, you get my point. Let's all say thanks.

4. Smile. Or Get Botox

In 2008, researchers in the United Kingdom noticed a strange phenomenon. Patients who had gotten Botox in their foreheads reported feeling fewer negative feelings and more positive ones. The trend was so overwhelming the researchers thought perhaps they could use Botox to treat depression. After a bit more digging, they found the positive feelings weren't caused by a chemical reaction; they were caused by people's inability to frown.

No joke! People weren't able to crease their foreheads and make grumpy frowning faces, and thus people around them weren't frowning back! Researchers labeled it a "lack of negative mood feedback."

You may not even be aware of the signals you're sending out into the world. People have a tendency to unknowingly mimic the nonverbal cues they get from other people. You frown, they frown. You smile, they smile. If you happen to have a face that naturally looks a little bit, well, crabby, you might want to make a conscious effort to turn that frown upside down.

5. Slow Down

I don't know about you, but I get anxious and angry when I'm on a tight schedule (or I'm hungry or have to pee. Sorry, too much information). Taking time to take care of ourselves is essential if we want to draw more kindness into our lives and ward off the onset of negativity. I find peace in my life when I find space. I don't necessarily need space from people, but I certainly need to allow my schedule to breathe a little. I enjoy arriving early to events so I can get myself settled. I enjoy leaving a short gap between appointments so I don't have to rush from one thing to another. A tiny five-minute window creates enough margin in my day for both giving and receiving kindness.

The perfect example of this happened in my own life when I went to a Little Caesar's drive-thru to pick up some pizzas for a birthday party. The kids had all arrived at the park and it was my job to go grab the pizza. I was in no rush because the longer I stayed away, the longer someone else could be in charge of wrangling the children.

I pulled up to the window and was greeted by a bored-looking young woman. This was not her dream job, but to her credit she didn't roll her eyes when I asked if I could wait while she cooked fresh pizzas for us (instead of getting whatever might be under the heat lamp). "No problem. Drive back through in ten minutes and we'll have them ready," she replied. I expressed my gratitude, and she gave me a half-smile.

Before I knew it, more words flew out of my mouth. "You have a beautiful smile." She smiled even brighter, and I drove off.

Ten minutes later I was back in that drive-thru to grab my fresh, hot pizzas. This time, the cashier smiled as she handed over the boxes. "Here's a bag with plates and napkins for you," she said, "and I threw in some cookies for dessert."

Taking that little bit of time to really see and connect with the person in front of me brightened both of our days (and, bonus, got me some free cookies!), but it wouldn't have happened if I had been in a grab-and-go sort of mood.

Make some space in your life so you can avoid the rush. Slowing down helps us to create and receive kindness.

6. Offer a Word of Encouragement to One Person Each Day

As children we stuck our tongues out at the playground bully and hollered with a fake bravado, "Sticks and stones may break my bones but words will never hurt me." We were wrong.

Wikipedia (you know I love me some Wiki) tells me this childhood rhyme has been around since 1862.[1] For over 150 years we have been telling ourselves that words don't matter. But they do.

A year after I had my third baby, a man at the gym said to me, "With as much as you work out, I'd think you'd be thin by now." I punched him as hard as I could in the face and then walked away.

Sorry, that was my inner meanie talking. I may have wanted to punch him, but instead I laughed good-naturedly and made a comment about my love for chocolate, then walked away with my head high but feeling a touch wounded.

Mean words hurt. They stick. But kind words stick too.

I remember the boy in elementary school who spoke up in music class the day I was too scared to try out for the musical. I wanted the part of Dorothy, but I was too shy to actually sing about any rainbows. In front of twenty third-grade classmates,

Dean Zavadsky bravely spoke up and said, "It's okay, Nicki. Just sing it. We promise not to laugh at you."

I sang the song and got the part. Many years later I would represent the state of Wisconsin by singing on stage at the Miss America Pageant. I wonder if Dean even remembers the way he breathed encouragement into a young classmate's heart that day? Nearly four decades later, I still remember.

I've been the recipient of many words of encouragement throughout the years, so I assume everyone has a similar circle of personal cheerleaders, but that's not actually always the case.

I recently received a message from a woman who goes to my church. I don't actually know her very well. I have only spoken to her one time in passing. She told me I could share her note with you, in hopes of illustrating the impact of one kind word.

> Hi, Nicole, I have wanted to tell you something for a long time. The day you and your husband were confirmed into our church, you gave me a compliment. You simply said, "That color looks beautiful on you." Please don't think I'm a whiner, but rarely do I receive compliments about my looks, particularly from a stranger. I think I might have given you an odd look because I thought "Why is this stranger being nice?" I guess I was suspicious because people who are that nice to me usually want something. At least that's what I used to think. As time passed I learned what a truly genuine person of faith and kindness you are. Therefore, I began to feel bad about the look I gave you.
>
> My husband and I have welcomed our first grandchild into the world, and I have retired from my business to pursue other interests, both professional and personal. You have impacted me more than you will ever know. Your one sentence of kindness has truly changed my life.

Can you imagine the rush of love I felt when reading this message? We all have times, like I did standing in the church that day, when a lovely thought flickers into our minds. *That woman looks so beautiful in that color.* Do we keep it to ourselves, wasting an easy opportunity to brighten someone's day, or do we give it away freely?

Sticks and stones may break our bones, but the power of words is also in our control. Will our words be the gift that quenches a thirsty soul or the dagger that hits an already hurting heart? Or will we simply keep those encouraging words to ourselves because we're too shy or too busy to give them away?

When we lay our heads on our pillow each night, I think it's important to be able to name the effect we made on another person that day.

The woman at church sure did light up when I told her she looked beautiful in that color. The woman on the phone sure sounded pleased when I told her I couldn't have resolved my shipping issue without her. My child's teacher sure did look delighted when I told her how much Ben enjoys having her as a teacher.

I am constantly learning from the ways other people do kindness. Sarah, the marketing guru on my "kindness team"—the group of women who help keep my life and business in order—called FedEx to tell them how grateful she was the delivery driver had carried her big, heavy bag of dog food all the way up to the front door instead of leaving it in the driveway. Sarah thought that was a really nice thing to do in the middle of winter, so she asked them to pass along a message of thanks to the driver.

A few days later, Sarah was pulling out of her very long driveway when a FedEx driver waved her down. Sarah thought maybe they had another package for her. Nope. The woman in the truck hopped out and ran over to Sarah's minivan. "Hey, are you the one who left the message?" she asked.

Sarah replied with a smile, "Are you the one who carried that super heavy dog food right to my front door?"

The driver said, "You have no idea how much your message meant to me that day. When my boss told me a comment had come in, I didn't believe him. He actually had to send me the screenshot. Thank you for leaving that message."

When Sarah told me about the interaction, she ended with, "I learned her name is Bambi. She's our FedEx driver, and she wears a rainbow-colored stocking beanie. So now we're friends. I just happened to have a new copy of *Kindness Is Courageous* in the car, so now she's reading your book."

Ah, Sarah. Do you see why she's on the kindness team? And why she's the marketing guru? She's reeling them in, one unsuspecting FedEx driver at a time.

There you go: six ways to draw more kindness into your life. Doing any of these things will change your day and the day of the person who crosses your path. Once you get one habit down, add in another. You'll be shocked by how good you feel when you're able to banish the burden of negativity.

Questions to ponder while you're standing in line at the post office:

1. How am I already drawing kindness into my life using these six tips?
   - Expect people to be kind.
   - Look for the silver lining in every situation.
   - Verbalize your gratitude.
   - Smile. Or get Botox.
   - Slow down.
   - Offer a word of encouragement to one person each day.
2. Which one of these tips do I want to implement today? How, specifically, will I do that?

Saying No to the Negative

It would be a real shame to work so hard at drawing more kindness into our lives and then sabotage it all by falling into old habits. You might think to yourself, *Yes! I want to draw more kindness into my life. I'm going to say yes to kindness starting today!* Then you go to work tomorrow, walk into the break room, and find all of your colleagues vilifying your boss or another coworker. It's awfully uncomfortable to be the purveyor of kindness in a world of yuck—unless you have a plan. That's why we have to not only say yes to kindness but also say no to the negative.

When you walk into that break room tomorrow, people are going to expect you to behave the way you behaved yesterday. If you had a tendency to jump in for the latest gossip, they are going to expect you to show up and chime in. They will not understand you have read this super amazing, life-transforming book about what happens when you say yes to kindness and are now driving down a completely different road.

We have to set ourselves up for success by anticipating what is coming and how we will handle it. Maybe it would help to first ask ourselves how we want to feel. Do we want to feel happy or unhappy? Do we want to feel like we got the last word? Is it important to feel justified even if it leaves us empty and cranky? It may seem like it's just the way we are made, like it's in our DNA to be sarcastic or doubtful of the good in the world, but it's not. We can retrain our brains. Let's look at six ways to get through the land mines of negativity.

1. Make a Decision to Stop Saying Negative Words

Negativity is habitual. It's a rut we dig for our brains through years of thoughtless comments. It's the easy way, but it's certainly not the way to happiness. We get to choose how we feel, but it has to start with a decision. We have to make the choice to take baby steps with our behavior each day that will eventually add up to more joy in our lives.

First, make a decision to stop saying negative words. It's like recovering from an addiction; you have to decide at some point that the way you've always done things in the past is not the way you want to do them in the future. You are essentially saying to yourself, *Enough is enough*, and truly and honestly acknowledging you have room for improvement when it comes to your thoughts and your words.

Studies show when people want to lose weight, they have more success when they physically write down and keep track of what they are putting in their mouths. The opposite is true for kindness. Instead of tracking what goes into our mouths, we need to track what's coming out. Start with a little self-monitoring. *Was that comment true? Was it helpful? Was it inspiring? Was it necessary? Was it kind?* In short, we want to T.H.I.N.K. when we speak: True, Helpful, Inspiring, Necessary, Kind. This little acronym is on posters in classrooms across the United States. I first used it when I was putting together a presentation for elementary school students, but I've found it also works well for adults.

2. Get an Accountability Partner

Sometimes we can't hear ourselves. We get so used to just doing things the way we've always done them and saying the things we've always said that we can't hear what we're saying. We are in a rut, and it's jeopardizing our true happiness.

Let's say you are playing golf. I am going to learn to play golf when I am sixty and all the kids are out of the house. Until then, I will continue to drive past golf courses while I taxi my kids to their 642 extracurricular activities. The few times I have played golf, I spent the entire time telling anyone within earshot how bad I am at the game. "I'm sure I'm going to whiff this." "Watch out behind me; the ball will probably go backward."

I might not listen very well to others, but I sure do listen to myself. When I tell myself I'm going to be bad at something, I always prove myself right. Self-talk is dangerous when it's negative. If I had said, "I bet I'm going to be good at this game once I get the hang of it," I would have given myself the confidence to continue trying. Instead, I heard myself degrading my athleticism and, sure enough, whiffed it.

An accountability partner is someone who can hear what you're saying more clearly than you can. We may not realize in the moment the damage our words can do. We think we're being funny or protecting ourselves from criticism of others by beating them to the punch.

If you find yourself picking on yourself or others with your words, get an accountability partner. This should be someone you trust, who has your best interest at heart, and who is gentle but honest. Ask them to tell you when they hear you speaking

63

negatively. The conversation might go something like this: "Hey, I'm trying to work on being more positive toward myself and others. Sometimes I say things without even realizing what I'm saying. If you hear me being critical with my words, would you please gently point it out to me?"

3. Snap That Rubber Band

You know those cute rubber bracelets that people wear with sayings like "Live Strong" or "WWJD"? Yeah, this is not that. If you want to retrain your brain to back away from negativity, it's going to take something with a bit of elastic.

I wear a hair tie around my wrist all the time. I never know when I'll need it to pull back my luscious brunette locks. (Um, yeah, my hair is neither luscious nor actually brunette, but that's a story for another day.) I keep that rubber band on my wrist not only for my hair but also for my mind. When a negative thought creeps in uninvited, I snap that rubber band. I pull it far from my wrist and then let go. Yep, it hurts.

Snapping the rubber band is a physical reminder of the emotional pain we cause ourselves and others with our words. Trust me, it doesn't take too long for your mind and your body to work together. Physical pain is a powerful deterrent.

After a while you won't even need to snap the rubber band. Just wearing it will be enough. You'll become like my dog, Dakota. She's a Golden Doodle, which means she's smart and loves to chase things into the woods. We installed an invisible electric fence to keep her safe and to stop her from leaving her Doodle doo-doo in the neighbors' yards. Dakota caught on to the rules very quickly. She didn't want to experience the pain of crossing her boundaries. Well, the fence is broken. It hasn't worked for several years, but when we put the special collar around Dakota's neck, she still won't leave the yard. It's a physical reminder to her of the behavior that's expected of her.

Don't worry; when it comes to humans, old dogs can learn new tricks.

4. Use a Predetermined Exit Plan

Remember how I said, "When you walk into that break room tomorrow, people are going to expect you to behave the way you behaved yesterday"? They will expect you to gossip or complain or do whatever the "old" you did. That's why it's important to set ourselves up for success by anticipating what is coming and how we will handle it.

I once knew two women who were friends—until they weren't. Since I had reason to interact with both of them each week, it didn't surprise me when one of them called me. "Listen, Nicole," she started. "I just want to let you know that Michelle . . ." That's when I cut her off. "Hold on," I said. "I'm going to extend to Michelle the same kindness I would extend to you, and I'm not going to talk about her when she's not around. But I promise you, I won't talk about you when you're not around either."

The conversation went dead after that, but this woman knew where I stood, and it was smack dab in Switzerland, the neutral zone. We can become a guilty party just by agreeing to be on the listening end of negativity.

I had a group of preteen girls in my kitchen a few years ago when I noticed they'd all started talking about a classmate. I listened quietly for a few minutes until I just couldn't stand it anymore. The whole house felt like it was filling up with toxic energy. I stepped in gently, saying, "You all have known her for a long time. Tell me something good about her." They paused for a moment, and then every girl came up with something special about that classmate. The air in our house was breath-able again.

When you are in conversations you can't find a way out of, be the person who brings light into the situation. Or be the person who walks away.

Walk away, you say? Yes. Get up and go to the bathroom. Give yourself a moment alone to think about what role you want to play in the conversation. If all goes well, the group will have moved on to another topic by the time you return.

My family and I lived in a small town in Ohio for several years while my husband was coaching at the nearby university. The thing I learned quickly about this town is that everyone knows everyone. It's pretty cool. You never have to worry about what your kids are up to because someone will tell you if they're being naughty. Lots of ears in the cornfield.

The downfall is that many opinions were laid way before I joined the community. I wanted to be able to form my own thoughts about people based on my interactions with them, so I asked my new friends not to tell me any of the gossip. The one caveat was that they were allowed to tell me if anyone in my fam-ily was going to be in danger. It worked really well, and I would do it that way all over again, but it did take some occasional sidestepping.

One day I was at a restaurant with two friends when a woman I didn't know walked up to the table. She began talking to my friends about her distaste for a certain man in town. I could tell I didn't like the way the conversation was going, so I got up and went to the bathroom. By the time I got back to the table, the woman was gone. My friends were mortified. They apologized up and down for not being able to stop her from talking about this man. I told them not to worry about it, that it had nothing to do with them. I wasn't in the least bit upset; I just didn't want to hear what she was saying, so I excused myself.

Well, a few months later, my friends ran into that woman again and she was full of regret. "I can't get that interaction out of my head," she said. "I'm so embarrassed that I would rant on like that in front of Nicole. Can you please tell her I'm sorry?"

Honestly, if that woman were standing in front of me right now, I wouldn't be able to pick her out. I can't remember her name or what she looks like. That's how unbothered I was by that day. But here's the thing: none of us needed to call her out for her negative words. We don't need to be the gossip police and write tickets for offenders. We just have to do what feels right to us and our personal conscience. Eventually, our positivity will shine so brightly that others will notice for themselves and want to be like us.

I was at a speaking event when a woman in the audience said, "But Nicole, if we don't join in the conversation or we defend someone, everyone else will automatically assume we are taking sides. We can end up ostracized from the group."

The threat of being an outcast is a real thing. I think it's especially hard for teens, where "if you're not with us, you're against us" is a powerful force. Those high school years are rough. Whether you're dealing with a workplace or school situation, though, there is one argument that seems to make sense to people. It's this: "I'm working on myself right now. I can't afford to get caught up in what so-and-so is doing because I'm trying to create more happiness in my own life." There really is no comeback against someone who wants to bring more joy into their life, because isn't that what we're all trying to do?

5. Memorize a Mantra to Replace Negative Thoughts

If you feel like you're having déjà vu, don't panic. We mentioned mantras way back in chapter 2 when we talked about those hurry, worry, jury thoughts that keep us distracted from being kind. We mentioned we can only think one thought at a time, so it's important to both reject the negative thought and also replace it with something else. I told you about a little piece of paper I kept in my pocket with words I was trying to memorize. Any of that ring a bell?

The idea is to retrain our brain. We are so smart, and our bodies work so efficiently, that every day our mind is learning how to react to situations tomorrow based on how we react to them today. Those negative little thoughts are going to weasel their way in and try to grab hold for good so they can continue to berate us with feelings of hurt, self-righteousness, or worry. The sooner we can bring in the heavy-duty shop vac and suck them all up, the better. We do that by intentionally replacing grimy thoughts with ones that glimmer. Too cheesy? How about we replace dark thoughts with ones that are dazzling? Or icky thoughts with ones that are iridescent? Messy to magnificent? Sloppy to splendid? (Sorry, I got a little carried away with the thesaurus.) I'm pretty sure you get my point. Think about what you're thinking about, and know you have the power to change those thoughts.

6. Create Stories and Ask Questions with the Intent to Build Compassion

A man I know became friends with an older woman when he was doing some work on her house. She mentioned in passing that she sure wished she had a little TV for her kitchen, because that area of the house was awfully quiet. This guy didn't have a lot of money, but he wanted to get her a TV, so he did. The next thing he knew, the elderly woman's children had filed a restraining order against him. They had never met the man, but they assumed he was a con artist. Even if they had contacted him, I imagine their questions would have had a skeptical edge. *What do you want from our mother?* However, if they would have taken the time to make a phone call and have a discussion, they would have learned the man enjoyed spending time with their mom because she reminded him of his own mother, who had recently passed. He remembered how lonely his own mother would get in her house when it was too quiet. He saw a way to make things better for someone else, and he took it.

Questions that are accusations get us nowhere. Questions that are bridges to understanding get us everywhere. When we want to find kindness in the hard places, we have to first find compassion. Empathy and compassion grow when we step away from our fears and preconceived ideas and ask questions from a heart that simply wants to learn. When we are curious and trying to understand someone else's actions or point of view, we find forgiveness, restoration, and a softness toward people we may have previously judged as being "bad."

If you're trying hard to find common ground with someone, asking thoughtful questions can go far. When you get a snippy email from a coworker, instead of immediately putting them on the list of people you hate, how about taking a few seconds to walk over and survey the situation for yourself? You might even say, "That last email didn't sound like you. Is everything okay?" You may find out the person is hungry, tired, going through a tough time at home, or worried about a deadline. In short, you'll find out the tone of the email had nothing to do with you. You were simply collateral damage for something else going on in their life.

Sometimes asking questions is out of the question. I do not suggest following the person who cut you off in traffic until they stop at a gas station. Walking up to them and saying, "Hey, I noticed you cut me off back there. Is everything okay?" is a strong no-go.

So, then what? This is where creating stories is so important. That woman who lets the door slam in your face as you leave the rec center? Maybe she's not rude, just preoccupied. Instead of being offended, we can think to ourselves, *I bet she just registered her son for basketball camp and she's wondering if that check is going to bounce. Or how she's going to cut back on the grocery bill to cover the difference.*

This is key: we are never going to ask if our story is correct. It's not a matter of truly figuring out what is going on in someone's life. Creating stories is our tool to move our minds from a place of tension to a place of tenderness.

Let's try another scenario. You're in the cereal aisle when you see a mom with kids who are crawling all over the cart and knocking boxes off the shelf as they roughhouse their way past the Cap'n Crunch. It's easy to judge and think, *What's her problem? Why doesn't she get her hooligans under control?* But what else could you think to move your mind away from the negativity?

Maybe we could take a closer look at the mom and see the bags under her eyes. Then perhaps we might begin our story by imagining she didn't get any sleep last night because her husband told her he lost his job.

It doesn't matter if it's true or not. What matters is moving our minds away from the place of negative judgment so our hearts are open to kindness.

It even works on ourselves. I was sitting in a cold, sterile room at the breast cancer center waiting for my six-month checkup. I was told it would be a bit of a wait, but the nurse wanted me to put the white robe on so I would be ready as soon as the doctor was available. I waited ten minutes, then twenty, then thirty. I am not a patient waiter. Or a patient patient, you might say. I debated poking my head into the hallway and giving some nurse a dirty look and an exaggerated sigh. But then it occurred to me, *I don't have cancer! I had cancer, but they fixed it. Now all I have to do is show up every six months.* Some of the people sitting in that clinic were going to be told they had breast cancer that very day. Wouldn't I want the doctor to spend as much time as possible with them so they could leave feeling reassured?

I decided to imagine I wasn't in a cold clinic but instead at a fancy spa. I lay down on the table and took some deep breaths. I relished the quietness, the calmness.

When the doctor walked in, she was absurdly apologetic and totally perplexed that I wasn't the least bit angry after waiting ninety minutes. I told her about my imaginary spa day. The tension left her face and her shoulders, and she smiled. Then she gave me all the time I needed so I could leave the cancer center reassured, just like the rest of the patients.

Our brains desperately want to sit on autopilot, thinking the same old thoughts we've always thought. But then we end up feeling the same old way we've always felt. There is room for more happiness in our lives, but we have to intentionally choose to take steps each day to say no to the negative and draw more kindness into our lives.

Modifying our behavior with even a few of these steps helps us escape the ruts that have been building up for years and determining our level of happiness. We get to choose how we feel. If you want to be happier, make the choice to take steps each day with your behavior that will eventually add up to happiness.

Questions to ponder while you're waiting for the doctor:

1. How have I already said no to the negative using one of these six tips?
   - Make a decision to stop saying negative words.
   - Get an accountability partner.

- Snap that rubber band.
- Use a predetermined exit plan.
- Memorize a mantra to replace negative thoughts.
- Create stories and ask questions with the intent to build compassion.

2. Which one of these tips do I want to implement today? How, specifically, will I do that?

What Counts as Kindness

Are People Taking Advantage of You?

I hate buying presents for my husband. Christmas, birthdays, and Father's Day all have me breaking out in a cold sweat. The man has everything. He wants nothing. I wander around Walmart trying to decide if he'll use an electric neck massage pillow (he didn't) or a new pair of sunglasses (he did, until he lost them two days later). Buying gifts for my husband is no fun. This year I'm going to buy him a Rite Aid gift card, because every time we go there he gets caught up in the "As Seen on TV" aisle. I'm not even kidding.

The funny thing is, my girlfriends also have everything they could want or need, but birthday shopping for them is a totally different experience. I can spend an hour at Walmart and leave so excited and invigorated because I found the perfect ice bucket in which to put a beach towel and sunscreen, along with a few bottles of fancy flavored water.

So what's the difference? I'm still at Walmart spending money. Why does one feel like such a chore while the other fills me with joy?

Here's my philosophy on doing nice things: not everything counts as kindness. When it feels like a duty, it's an expectation. When it feels like a delight, it's kindness. Duty versus delight. It's important to get that into our heads, because those words will save us from people taking advantage of us in the name of "kindness."

Let's look at some more examples. You agree to make forty-seven batches of brownies for the school bake sale because you're on the PTA board and it feels like the right thing to do. Okay, so do it. But if you dread it, don't call it kindness.

On the flip side, your son's class is having a winter party and you decide it would be fun to make vegan, gluten-free, sugar-free snowman cookies for the entire school. Does that excite you? Then it's kindness.

Sometimes we have to do things that aren't very fun because it's expected of us. That's life. My friend's mother-in-law had this annoying habit of texting her every time it was a family member's birthday so she would remember to send them a card. It drove my friend nuts. "I can remember just fine on my own. I don't need someone to tell me to wish someone else a happy birthday," she said. It became a duty to reach out to the celebrant. Popping a card in the mail was a job on the to-do list, not an act of love. Knowing she had to do it took all the joy out of it, even though she actually does like to send birthday cards to let people know she's thinking of them.

Coincidentally, the mother-in-law stopped texting my friend these birthday reminders—and guess what, my friend forgot! She now wishes she had those reminders. At least when my friend does remember to send a card, it's because she wants to.

Think about your gut reaction to whatever activity is in front of you. If you roll your eyes or let out a groan, it's not kindness—at least not the kind of kindness I'm talking about, which fills you up and refreshes your mind and body.

My husband, Saul, and I met a woman several years ago who was living in poverty. No hot water, no car, sometimes no electricity. It was a dire situation. That first Christmas, I called and asked if I could help her buy presents for her kids. We were friends, so she and I went shopping together and picked out a few things. Then I went shopping on my own and found some extra presents to surprise this mom. It was fun! So fun! I loved being a part of their holiday and felt really honored that she would allow me into her life. I couldn't wait for them to open their gifts. I was more excited about Christmas morning than they were.

The next year, the same thing happened. So fun! The year after that, it was less fun. The next year it was even less fun. The fun started dwindling because I started to see my gift-giving as a duty. Resentment started creeping in, which means so did negativity. I began judging how the family spent their time and money, how quickly the presents I bought were chewed up by a dog or left on the front lawn. I had lost all delight in giving.

I got fed up one Christmas and ended up giving the family a gift card for food instead. I knew I was expected to do something, but I didn't want to spend my precious energy on something that felt like a big, fat waste of time. It wasn't kindness, because it didn't feel like kindness feels. It felt like a duty.

Looking back, I realize it was my fault. This family never asked me to create Christmas for them. I took it upon myself, but I held on to an expectation of how those gifts should be received and the thanks I should be getting. The mother had enough on her plate. She didn't have the capacity to try to make me feel good for being nice to her. I expected her to fill my emotional bucket when I really needed to manage my own emotional needs.

Maybe you've been in a situation like this, where an action started out by filling your cup but now it feels like a life sentence.

Or you were all excited to do something for someone only to be met by a total lack of gratitude. What do we do? How do we stop the bitterness that comes from feeling like someone is taking advantage of us? We have to make a choice.

When we reach this fork in the road, we have to decide to either stop the giving or get a new attitude about it.

Did you know you have the option to say no? Maybe you need permission to do this. If so, here you go. *You have the right to say no.*

In fact, we have a responsibility to prevent resentment by saying no or by saying yes on our terms. I would argue that we show much more kindness to our immediate family and friends when we protect ourselves from being drained by those "have to" things in life. You don't have to bake forty-seven dozen brownies. You can say no. You don't have to agree to teach Sunday school for the fifth year in a row. You can gracefully bow out. You don't have to run the concession stand at your daughter's volleyball games or be troop leader for the Girl Scouts or volunteer to coach your son's baseball team. And you certainly do not have to do all these things at the same time. How do I know? Because I've said no to all of those things in the past. I've lived through it, and people still give me credit for being kind.

My Bible study group recently read a book called *The Best Yes*.[1] We now call ourselves the BYGs, the Best Yes Gals. We hold each other accountable for making space in our lives to love others well. We do that by creating margins of free time by saying no. Only none of us ever says the word *no*. We've learned to say to people, "I'm sorry, but that's not my best yes right now." Even as a friend group, when one of us invites another to coffee, we will say, "I know you're busy, so this might not be your best yes, but do you want to meet at Starbucks?" Then the other person replies, "Of course!" because who doesn't want to ditch all responsibilities and meet with friends?

When we get grumpy about giving, we need to consider saying no. But in some situations, I realize saying no is not an option. If your mother-in-law is used to getting a birthday gift from you, you might want to keep doing that even if she's never happy with it or is always passive-aggressively critical about it. (By the way, for the record, I hit the jackpot when I got married. My mother-in-law is amazing. I'm talking about *your* mother-in-law here.)

What do we do when we have to keep giving but it's beginning to annoy us? We ditch the expectations. You know you can never change someone, right? We can hang around them and hope our awesomeness rubs off on them, but truly, we cannot change someone's words or actions. That's actually good news, because it means we also don't have to take responsibility for their words or actions. They control their attitude and we control ours.

When we bump up against someone impossible to please, holding on to that truth will set us free. Free from feeling hurt when they don't appreciate our effort. Free from judging what they do with the gift we have given them. Free from feeling like we are owed something in return.

My friend Cathy is a grandmother with a huge heart and a small bank account. She came across a woman at a gas station who asked for money to fill her tank. Cathy handed her a scarce $20 bill and wished her well. Instead of putting gas in her car, the woman drove away! Clearly that money was not going to be used for its original intention. As Cathy was telling me the story, she said, "There was a time when that would have made me mad. But I thought to myself, 'How would Nicole feel about this situation?' and I realized I have to give without any expectations. I wanted to be kind, so that's what I did."

Um, forgive me, but to answer the question, How would Nicole feel about this situation?, Nicole would be irate. I would have hopped into my car *Dukes of Hazzard* style, chased that liar down, and tackled her on the gravelly side of the road.

Sorry, that was my inner meanie talking.

I was touched that Cathy felt like she had a new perspective after hanging out with me. What a compliment. But more than her story building my ego, it was proof of what I've learned to believe: we can't control someone else's behavior, but we can control our own.

Back to that fork in the road. When we begin to feel like someone is taking advantage of us, we either say no or we let go of our expectations and therefore change our perspective. We can also change our perspective by bringing creativity and gratitude into the situation.

Let's start with creativity. Creativity ignites fun. Fun plus doing something nice equals kindness. Whoa! Hold the phone. What is being nice? Isn't it the same as being kind? Nope. In my brain, there is a big difference. Being nice is being good. It's following the rules and doing what you're supposed to do. *Be a nice boy. Nice girls don't do that.* Being nice is great. I strive to be nice all the time, but it's more of a general idea of how people expect us to act based on our cultural norms. To me, being kind is a little friskier and riskier. We choose to be kind when we do something that might take us a bit out of our comfort zones or when we go beyond what we're expected to do. Fun plus nice equals kindness (on the contrary, dread plus nice equals duty). We want to make giving fun, even when it's something we have to do, because if we have fun doing it, it's never a waste of time or resources.

My daughter, Jordan, loves to sew. Lately she's been on a quilting kick. We won't see our teenager for an entire weekend, and then Sunday night she will descend from her upstairs lair with an original Jordan Phillips creation. I don't know what kind of magic she's spinning up there, but she comes downstairs with the most soft and colorful quilts you have ever seen. Sometimes she knows who the recipient will be, and other times she doesn't. She could hand it off to her arch nemesis (if she had one) who would throw her head back and laugh wickedly—and it wouldn't matter much, because Jordan had a blast making it. I'm sure there are Jordan Phillips creations sitting on the floor of people's closets or lining their garbage cans, but Jordan never thinks of that. The kindness high she gets comes from the creative process and from thinking about how much the recipient might enjoy the colors and textures, not from someone else's actual appreciation or lack thereof.

What do you love to do? Do you love to shop? Then go spend an hour collecting things that bring you joy and turn them into a gift. When I had cancer, someone sent me a box of sunshine. Everything in the box was yellow: yellow soap, a yellow washcloth, a yellow candle, yellow party decorations. I could feel happiness exuding from the box, not only because of the cheerful color but also because I could imagine how picking out those things must have filled this woman's creative spirit.

If you love to paint, do that. No one expects you to be a Picasso. And we're not worrying about others' expectations, right? If you love to go for long walks on the beach, do that. I had a woman send me a box of heart-shaped rocks. It must've cost her a fortune to mail them across the United States, but as I looked at each one of them, I could imagine the delight she felt as she came across each perfectly shaped treasure. She has no idea what I've done with those rocks. That wasn't her concern. She loved finding the rocks and sharing them. What might come next wasn't on her mind. She let go of expectations and let her creativity fly.

In all of these examples, people are being filled up by gift-giving because they are combining fun with niceness. It's nice to send someone a gift when they are going through cancer, but it refreshes us at the same time when we are doing a little bit more than what is expected or doing it a little bit differently. We can also get those feel-good kindness chemicals flowing by combining gratitude with niceness.

Check out this fancy equation: gratitude plus niceness equals kindness.

Let's say you have agreed to serve food at a homeless shelter. That might be fun and fulfilling, until some fellow goes through the line and complains that you're serving spaghetti *again*. You think to yourself, *Listen, pal, I don't have to be here serving you right now. I could be home on my couch eating ice cream. You should be grateful.* That is something my inner meanie would say. If we want to keep our minds in a place that is calm and un-offended, the only person who needs to get grateful is us. Not to repeat myself, but we can't control someone else's words or actions. We can only control our own.

Gratitude can take many forms in our minds. We can be grate-ful we aren't the one going through the dinner line at the home-less shelter. We can be grateful we aren't the one with a drug habit. We can be grateful our mother-in-law went through painful labor to give birth to our amazing husband. We can be grateful that amazing husband goes to work and earns a paycheck even though he can't figure out how to put his gross socks in the dirty laundry bin. We can even look at someone and be grateful we don't have the anger, resentment, or crummy attitude they are displaying.

Distinguish between duty and delight. Ask yourself, *How do I feel about doing this?* Then make a decision to either say no or change your expectations. You can change your expecta-tions by adding some creative fun to the situation or by getting grateful. Creativity and gratitude ignite delight. When delight is ignited, we have full-fledged kindness that refreshes and reinvigorates our bodies and leaves us wanting to give even more.

Questions to ponder while you're wandering through Walmart:

1. What things in your life need the boot because they aren't really filling your soul?
2. Would it be better to say no to those things, or do you need to give yourself an attitude adjustment?

When Kindness Isn't about You

Have you ever stopped to consider that perhaps the world doesn't revolve around you? I know, you probably haven't heard that line since you were a teenager. Me neither. Sometimes I need to drag it out and run it through my egocentric filter.

Like when someone steals my perfect parking place. I have to tell myself, *The world doesn't revolve around you, Nic.* Or when the Miracle suit I want (that's a swimsuit for moms who want to look ten pounds thinner) is backordered until August. *The world doesn't revolve around you, Nic.* Or when I want something done yesterday, but no one is willing to get to it until a week from Thursday. *The world doesn't revolve around you, Nic.*

I get it. I get it. Not everything is about me and my wants and needs, even when it comes to kindness.

If someone were to call and offer to pick up a gallon of milk for you at the grocery store today, what would you say? "No thanks, I've got it."

If someone were to call and offer to take your kids for the night so you could have a date with your husband, what would you say? "No, I don't want to trouble you."

If someone were to offer to bring you a meal this evening so you could have a night off from cooking, what would you say? "Nah, I don't want you to go through the hassle."

What if I were to tell you that in every one of those circumstances the world doesn't revolve around you? Maybe those acts of kindness were offered as a way for someone else to get out of their own head.

We've talked about all those feel-good chemicals that travel through our bodies when we are the giver, the receiver, or the witness of an act of kindness. If a person is in need of a boost to their day, and they aren't seeing kindness around them, they have to create it. They reach out to you and say, "Hey, can I help with . . . ?" I don't know about you, but I'm guilty of saying no as a knee-jerk reaction.

Why do we do that? Is it because we don't want to feel indebted to someone? Is it because we don't think they could do it as well as us? Is it because we don't want the hassle of explaining to them how something should be done? Is it because we don't want to put them out?

I completely changed my tune after I met a woman named Tammy Joy Lane.[1] Tammy is a veteran, a mom, and a kindness advocate. She has spent years battling bipolar depression, suicidal thoughts, and post-traumatic stress disorder.

Tammy once explained her journey to me like this:

Have you ever wondered what could be so bad that someone could take their own life? I have struggled with suicidal thoughts since I was in junior high. Now 20 years later, in my 33rd year, the suicidal thoughts have built a super highway in my brain. Let me break that down for you.

When a person without a suicide super highway gets negative feedback, they brush it off, learn from it and move on. For me, I go right to "I should kill myself."

When a person without a suicide super highway gets in a fight with their family, they know it will pass, they learn from it and move on. For me, I go right to "I should kill myself."

When a person without a suicide super highway drops a glass and breaks it, they clean it up. For me, I go right to "I should kill myself." It's not in a poor me, I need attention, nobody loves me kind of way. It's real. It's scary. It's overwhelming.

Every day I battle this. Every moment I have to distract myself from this and I never know what will be the trigger. So when I call you to see if I can help you, I'm probably just needing a break from myself. It's not always about you, so please say yes.[2]

The world doesn't revolve around us. Sometimes people are offering to help us paint a room or weed a garden or taxi children simply because they need to get out of their own space. They need a distraction from their own lives and a way to connect with others. They need to feel powerful and important, and kindness can give them that feeling.

Tammy has found that reaching out to others with kindness helps her escape some of those dark thoughts. She offers her kindness as a means of self-preservation.

When I had breast cancer in 2015, most days I would wake up and greet the day with gratitude. Then there were those other days. I'm sure you've had them. You wake up and the dreary, gray, rainy day seems to reflect what you're feeling in your heart. Why even bother to get out of bed? *Would it really matter if I just pulled the covers over my head and blocked out the world?*

As a mom of three, I couldn't afford to spend too much time in my pity party. The grocery store, dry cleaner, and post office were calling. It is possible to run our errands with a terrible attitude. We've all seen people do it. But I don't want to be one of those people who makes everyone else's day crummy because I'm in a funk.

That's where kindness comes in. Instead of blindly walking through the day, I would pick up a two-liter of Mountain Dew for my neighbor or buy a silly magnet for a friend or bake cookies for my kids to enjoy as a special after-school snack. I did something kind to reroute my day.

I remember one day in particular when I was feeling especially low. I rolled over and looked at the clock. It said 4:25 a.m. It was way too early to be awake, but the rain was coming down hard. Between the booming thunder and my hamster wheel thoughts, I figured there was no way I was going back to sleep.

I lay in bed and started thinking about the woman who was living in a tent in my neighbor's yard. She had finished a drug treatment program and was working hard to stay clean. She had a job at a dry cleaner across town. With no money and no car, she had no choice but to get up two hours before she needed to clock in and walk to work. Rain or shine, she got up at 4:30 a.m. to begin her trek.

There I was in the early morning hours thinking about Dawn (the woman, not the sunrise). A thought flitted through my brain. *Maybe I should get up and drive her to work.*

Raise your hand if you think I got out of bed to help her. Put your hand down. No way was my inner meanie going to allow me to get involved in an early morning taxi service. I rolled over and somehow fell back to sleep.

About two o'clock that afternoon, I was driving home when I noticed Dawn walking along the side of the road. I pulled over and offered her a ride. She declined, but before she walked away I added, "Are you still walking to work every morning?"

The minute those words were out of my mouth, I regretted it. I wanted to gather them all back in. I had no idea what I was about to offer if she said yes.

"Yes," she replied, "but I'm saving up for a bike, so pretty soon I'll ride to work and that will save me a lot of time."

Wait. She needed a bike? I had a bike. It was sitting in my garage feeling used and rejected because no one would ride it. I told Dawn I had a bike she could have. She just needed to come over to my house and claim it.

That afternoon, Dawn walked to the edge of my driveway. I rolled out the bike, and she paused before saying, "This will be great. I'll be sure to get it back to you as soon as I've saved enough money to buy my own."

She looked even more hesitant when I told her I didn't want her to borrow the bike, I wanted her to accept the bike as a gift. I could see the war waging in her mind. She knew she needed it, but the pride of accepting something from a near stranger felt very foreign and wrong. Eventually, with a little moisture in her eyes, she rode away on her new bike.

Dawn didn't want to accept my kindness. It killed her to have to rely on another person. What she didn't know is that I needed her to accept my kindness. She was a life preserver for me that day. Nothing could shake my depressed mood, and it was threatening to overtake my family.

Dawn had no way of knowing at the time that kindness didn't just come to her rescue. Her willingness to say yes allowed kindness to come to my rescue.

I'll be honest; sometimes we find ourselves in spots where the kindness of others seems a little overwhelming.

I've had several friends diagnosed with dumb diseases (I sort of think all diseases are dumb; I wish they'd just go away already). In each case, the outpouring of love comes flooding into their homes in a tidal wave. Food trains, phone calls, and flowers are hard to juggle when you're looking down the barrel of four months of chemotherapy. I can see it in their eyes, this overwhelming and panicky feeling that says, *How am I ever going to thank all these people?*

Way back when my high school daughter was a first-grader, she had a special friend whom she liked to refer to as her boyfriend. Ah, young love! This adorable little boy was diagnosed with leukemia. He missed tons of school but his parents sent a stuffed monkey in his place so the class could take pictures of all the activities they were doing and he could feel like part of the action. He had chemo and radiation and lost all of his hair. He had to quit playing hockey and doing all the other things he and his siblings loved doing together.

I visited with his mom a few times (you know, because our kids were dating), so I sort of had an inside scoop into what was happening in their home. Fellow parents set up a meal train, hockey moms raised money to cover the time off of work, and then the big one came: a silent auction at the school.

Word got out the PTA was organizing a neighborhood-wide silent auction to raise funds to help with medical expenses. Of course, we were all on board. Who wouldn't want to help this sweet family during the most difficult time of their lives?

Moms, dads, and teachers jumped into action, making it their mission to coordinate efforts. We were all excited to finally have some big way to contribute to this family. That's when I got the call.

The mom of this young boy begged me to contact the PTA and call it all off. "Please, Nicole, can you tell them to stop?" I can still hear the weariness in her voice as she told me she just couldn't stand being indebted to one more person. "There is nothing we can ever do to return all these favors."

I'd like to say I was able to convince her that these favors never needed a single thank-you, but that's not the way it went down. I called the PTA and told them this was all too much for the family to handle. They didn't want any more attention. They simply needed to be left alone so they could huddle up together and restore some normalcy to their lives.

Thankfully, they did get their normal back. The little boy was eventually able to return to the classroom, and he is now a cancer-free hockey-playing high schooler. (In case you're wondering, he and my daughter broke up in second grade once they realized the opposite sex has cooties.)

So, why would I use a chapter on accepting the kindness of others to tell the story of someone who didn't? Several reasons.

If someone doesn't seem to want your help, try to think about how overwhelmed they may feel. They might not care to be the center of attention and long to bring some normalcy to their lives. Your gift in that case might be to tell them you care and move away a bit. Try checking in again in a month or so to see if circumstances have changed.

I have found through my experiences on both sides of the helping issue that certain words bring more stress than others. When people say, "Let me know how I can help," or "Call me if you need anything," it becomes my job to include them. That's too much work when I'm already down and out, so I just never call. I much preferred when people would say, "If it's okay with you, I'll bring you milk, bread, and eggs. I'm going to the grocery store anyway. Need anything else?" Now, when I'm helping others who are going through a trying time, I try to be very specific: "I'm picking up my daughter at swim practice, so I'd love to bring your son home at the same time." Thinking of ways we can lighten someone's burden means they don't have the extra burden of thinking of things themselves.

If you are the one who is feeling indebted by the kindness being showered on you, you're not alone. When I had cancer, people kept asking if they could bring food over. My response was always no. I had a gluten allergy, my kids were picky eaters, my husband didn't want to answer the door—I had a million reasons for saying no. Then one day I realized all these people just loved me. They wanted to take away the cancer, but since they couldn't do that, they figured they'd cook. By saying yes to their food, I was allowing them to be part of my healing. If you find yourself in that situation and truly don't want to deal with people, designate one friend who can collect the meals for you or who can gently suggest an alternative, such as that maybe take-out gift cards would be a better option.

Not all acts of kindness require a thank-you note. If you're saying no to kindness because you feel too tired to reply to every card, gift, and errand, please know there are (in my humble opinion) times in which you can just sit back and be loved on. Dumb diseases, loss of a spouse or child, and any other thing that knocks your world completely down are all good reasons *not* to send a thank-you note. You do not need to repay kindness. It is given from the heart and therefore requires no effort on your part. Someday you'll be feeling better and then you can do something nice for someone else (without expecting a thank-you card). If you want to let someone know you're especially touched by their thoughtfulness, hand your cell phone to someone else in the family and have them send a short text.

We need to go back to that teenage adage and remember the world doesn't revolve around us. When we're going through a tough time and people want to help, we let them. It's going to make them feel like a good human, and it's going to keep their inner meanie quiet for at least a few hours. Helping others reassures people if and when they are going through a rough spot, someone will be there to help them too. And if you find yourself wanting to help someone who is having a hard time saying yes, understand it's not about you.

Questions to ponder when someone wants to bother you by bringing your kid home from practice or making you some chicken noodle soup:

1. Are there times I tell people no when I could easily say yes? Why do I do that?
2. What can I do to remind myself the kindness someone is offering may be a way to reroute their own bad day?

Being Kind in Your Home and Other Places Where People Annoy You

Let's say you wake up in the morning and the living room looks like someone had a kegger (that's a beer party, for anyone not from Wisconsin). There's a plate holding stale pizza crust, a few pieces of gross-smelling apparel at the foot of the couch, and a pile of used tissues on the end table. Your kids are moving like sloths even though it's a school day and everyone knows they need to be out of the house in ten minutes. Fifteen minutes later, you find them sitting on the couch looking at their electronic devices. You are busting it to get out the door only five minutes late when one child realizes he hasn't brushed his teeth yet and another screams that she can't possibly go to school because she has a test today and she completely forgot to study.

How's your day going? By 8:00 a.m. you are done. You've already spent your daily allowance of energy. The words spewing from your mouth aren't nearly as bad as the ones in your head that are threatening to escape.

Feeling like a pretty great parent, right? Yeah, not so much.

Home is where the heart is, but it's also where the heart of our problem often lies. We can be a very kind person to everyone we meet out in the real world, but the moment we walk in our own door, the mask comes off and our inner meanie is allowed to play.

When the morning starts off in a rush of tension, we carry that strain into our day. When we fight with our spouse or kids in the evening, it translates into a terrible night of sleep or a general yucky feeling. It's not just families who deal with this sort of unpleasantness. Anyone who lives with anyone can attest to the difficulty of having someone in your space. This is a big problem, because if you're not happy in your home, you're not truly happy anywhere. Kindness at home sets the tone for the day and for how you'll sleep at night.

Saul and I lived together before we were married. I know, we are terribly hedonistic people. In theory, living together seemed like the most exciting thing ever. I adored Saul, and still do. He was my childhood crush at age twelve, so to think I was his girlfriend at age twenty-four was just the best. We both knew we would get married within the next year, and financially living together seemed to make perfect sense since we were both dirt poor. We were young and in love and all that mattered was being together.

We quickly found out that even when you really, really love someone, too much togetherness can be a breeding ground for annoyance. For instance, Saul annoyed me when he refilled the ice cube trays even when there were still some cubes in them. *How do I get the old cubes out without getting all wet in the process?* I annoyed Saul when I used the last of the ice cubes.

Saul annoyed me when he snored. I annoyed Saul when I began my personal dance party at 6:00 a.m. Saul annoyed me when he left his socks on the floor. I annoyed Saul when I constantly harped at him about it.

We got married, added three children to the mix, and spent a good ten years getting more and more annoyed with each other. Sure, we were still young and in love, but there came a point when it felt like we didn't really like each other. I vividly remember the day I said, "Enough."

Saul was a head coach for the first time in his life. I was a television anchor working evenings and nights. (Carly was the babysitter who saved the day every day.) We had just spent the weekend together as a family doing fancy things like going to Menard's. I had made a comment about how he should put the shopping cart away differently than he was doing it, and he rolled his eyes at me. Something about that eye roll got me.

The following week we were once again on opposite schedules. I knew I needed to have a long talk with my husband, but I didn't want to do it face-to-face, because (1) that always escalated into a very loud "conversation," and (2) Saul was a better debater than me, so I knew I'd walk away feeling like I'd lost the argument. Besides, Saul was heading out for a series of road games. We didn't even have time to talk. Before I left for work that day, I sat down, wrote him a seven-page letter, and put it on top of his suitcase.

The letter basically said, "I love you, but I don't like you, and I'm pretty certain you don't like me anymore either. We agreed long ago never to use the word *divorce* and to work things out for better or worse, so I'm not saying we should separate, but I am saying I can't go on like this any longer. Something has to change."

Then I proceeded to tell him I had turned in a letter of resignation to my station's news director. Our little home was a teakettle and it was about to blow. I had to do what I could to release some of the pressure, so I decided to stop worrying about what was fair and simply support my husband.

Saul called me immediately, and instead of saying, "No, don't quit your job! Take back your letter of resignation," he said, "Thank you." Things changed almost overnight. I realized I wasn't the only one feeling stress. My stress came from trying to run a household via sticky notes to babysitter Carly, but Saul's stress was also immense. He was trying to pay our mortgage through the very public wins and losses of a bunch of guys on a basketball court. I began to see we were both worn out. It wasn't just about me and the way I felt I was being treated. We were in this together.

I was still heavily drinking at that time in our lives, so everything wasn't completely rosy, but our relationship turned a corner. Having a little less stress in our house made a big difference. We didn't argue about the dishes in the sink or who should remember to take out the garbage. We just each did what we could. I had more time to take care of household things. Once Saul found his groove as a head coach, he was happy to support my dream of traveling and teaching others about kindness. It took a little while to strike the perfect balance, and I definitely had a lot of personal growth I needed to do, but we found our way back to the life we had always wanted.

Perhaps you're thinking, *Sure, Nicole, good plan, but not everyone can quit their job.* Yep. That's true. But every one of us can trim some fat from our schedules. Instead of being in a constant state of go-go-go, we can be people who learn there is great kindness in saying no-no-no. As we discussed in chapter 6, learning to say no guilt-free not only keeps people from taking advantage of us but also means there is plenty of reserve left in the tank for those people who need us the most.

Outline Expectations

Why are the people you live with annoying you? My guess is that it's because they are not doing something you expect them to do. Expectations are dangerous things. I clean the house; I expect the family to respect my hard work and keep it clean. They don't know that is an expectation of mine and therefore get confused when Mount Saint Mommy explodes about the crumbs on the counter.

Problems with a roommate? I bet you expect them not to play their music at all hours or bring a boyfriend home for three-day snuggle fests. Maybe you expect them to clean the bathroom without being asked. You might look at these things as common sense or common courtesy, but what is common to you might be very foreign to a person who grew up with a different set of rules and guidelines. That's why we have to state our expectations early on. It doesn't have to be a tyrannical, tension-filled talk, just a simple, friendly conversation that says, "Hey, how do you feel about setting Monday as the day we clean the bathroom? We can switch off each week, and if one of us doesn't get it done by Monday at midnight, we owe the other frozen yogurt." Don't assume. State your expectations and ask your roommate what he or she expects from you.

In a family, this can be done with chore charts and specific house rules. "Here is the list of things we need to do every day. You can put a sticker on the chart when you finish. Ten stickers mean a special family game night." My older kids created a contract when they got their first phones. It was a clear-cut list of what was acceptable in our house and what would happen if those rules were broken.

If it's your spouse who's annoying you, think about what specifically gets under your skin. Does he or she not reply to your text messages? (My husband is guilty of that.) Do they start barking out the to-do list the minute you walk in the door? (I might be guilty of that.) Taking time to restate your expectations and asking your spouse to do the same can give you both a glimpse into how you can add kindness to your relationship. After several weeks of being annoyed at my husband, I finally said, "Why don't you ever answer my text messages?" He said he felt like he didn't need to since I wasn't asking a question. He didn't realize the lack of response made me feel insignificant. I learned from

Saul that he needs a few minutes to unwind after work before I start asking him questions or reminding him of what's on the schedule for the night. He can be kind by responding to my texts and I can be kind by giving him some space.

Create Space in Your Schedule

If mornings are a stressful time of the day for your family, train yourself and your kids to get up fifteen minutes earlier. I had to ban all electronics in the morning, including the television, because my kids would enter a zombie-like state and forget to eat their Cheerios.

When at all possible, leave five minutes early for everything. I'm a big fan of trying to do one more thing before I run out the door. Throw in one more load of laundry. Put one more dirty plate in the dishwasher. Feed the dog, clean the living room. There is always one more thing to do. I still fight that habit, but I've tricked myself and my family into being on time by changing the clocks in our house so they always run fast. When we stop hurrying, we start hearing. We can listen to the story our second-grader wants to tell us about turtles. We have the brain capacity to remember the bake sale brownies. We know who needs $20 for school fees, and if we don't have it, we have time to go through an ATM. Play with the timetable in your household and I bet you'll immediately notice a difference in your own level of kindness.

Check In Frequently

One day my husband asked me out of the blue, "How are we doing?" This was, shall I say, out of character for my dear love. In fact, I wasn't sure if he actually wanted an answer because he mushed the sentence together and actually said, "How we doin'?" But I digress. In answer to his question, I said, "Okay, I guess." That got his attention. "What do you mean, 'okay'?" he asked. This was midway through our marriage, and I was still being a flirtatious wife so I would always tuck a card or love letter in his suitcase when he left for road trips. But he never acknowledged them. Like never. Didn't say anything on the phone, didn't write one back, didn't bring them home and store them in a cute keepsake box. Nada.

"I just feel like I put forth the effort to tell you I love you in these cards and you don't really care."

He got quiet. And then he got truthful. "That's not really my thing. You put a lot of effort into them, but I'm sort of in the basketball zone when I'm out of town."

"So, it's okay if I stop hiding cards in your suitcase?"

"Yep."

Just like that, I felt a whole lot closer to my husband, because instead of getting annoyed that he was ignoring my gestures, I understood there were better ways to love him. Through many other "How we doin'?" conversations, we have resolved a lot of potential pitfalls in our marriage.

Maybe you don't ask your roommate, "How we doin'?" That could be weird. But there are words you can use to get the same result. It's a matter of intentionally checking in. "Is everything about us being roommates working for you, or is there something I can do that would make your life easier?"

I also suggest checking in with your kids. Every once in a while, I'll ask, "Is there anything I can do to make you feel more loved and supported as your mom?" Sometimes they say no, and sometimes they tell me I need to detach from my phone. Ouch.

That brings up the next point. You have to determine ahead of time how you're going to react to the answers to these questions.

When They Go Low, We Go High

I have to give credit to Michelle Obama for coming up with the statement, "When they go low, we go high." I see it as the perfect reminder to keep our wits about us when someone picks a fight. Stay even-tempered. Allow the conversation to unfold without raising our voices or spewing bitter comebacks. Unfortunately, that didn't happen when my kids told me I needed to spend less time on my phone. I got defensive immediately. *I have to use my phone for work. It's important I respond to people quickly. I don't use it that often. It's usually just sitting in the kitchen.* When my husband jumped in and took the kids' side, I got mad. Fortunately, when I went low, they went high. They brushed off my instant bad mood, knowing I'd need some time to self-reflect.

How about when it's the kids who go bonkers? This annoys me. I give and give and give, then I ask them to unload the dishwasher and it's an instant whine fest. (Not always, but sometimes.) Or one of them asks to go to a coed sleepover and I say no. Stomping. Words flying around, like, "You never let me do anything. All my friends' parents are letting them go." It's so easy to lift our weapons and shoot back when we're in the line of fire. Keeping our cool is hard, but it's essential. Kids need us to demonstrate how to navigate overflowing emotions. When we start screaming because they are whining over the dishwasher or slamming the door in our faces, the situation escalates. When we state the facts and agree to talk with them when they can hold a quiet conversation, we bring kindness into our homes. I sometimes feel like I need to reprimand them on the spot for being disrespectful, but that comes later. When everyone is calm, we can dole out consequences if needed.

When we ask tough questions, we are often given tough answers. Your spouse, roommate, or child might react explosively. We have to determine ahead of time if we are going to get sucked into that vortex or if we're going to remain levelheaded.

Give Grace

My friend Andrea (the one who told me to write this book) is a really good mom. Like really good. In my opinion, she has struck the perfect balance between guiding her children and giving them space. Her home has clear-cut rules, and she and her husband follow through on discipline instead of just threatening it. Well, even great moms with great teenage daughters can go through trying times. Andrea and her daughter, Peyton, have been traversing a sticky spot lately. Andrea feels like her daughter is becoming increasingly disrespectful, and Peyton feels like she can't walk into the room without her mom nagging her about something. Andrea realized they both had a point, but neither knew how to bridge the gap that was quickly becoming a chasm.

After a particularly tense morning, Andrea cleared her afternoon schedule. An hour before the school day was over, she went to the high school and had the office call her child down. Peyton was confused when she saw her mom and became more confused when she heard her mom say, "Get your stuff. We're going shopping!" What? Andrea went on to explain that she could feel the division growing between them and just wanted to spend a fun afternoon with her daughter, reminding her how much she loved her. That day was a game changer. Are things perfect now? Nope. But mother and daughter both appreciate the renewed kindness they feel in their home.

When it comes to being kind in our homes and to people who annoy us, give grace. Sometimes we need to clean up the plate we didn't get dirty. Sometimes we need to sit in the car for five minutes and just breathe before we walk in the door. Sometimes we need to remind ourselves we weren't the only one who had a stressful day. Kids have bad days, roommates have bad days, spouses have bad days.

There are times to remind someone of a chore they haven't done and there are times we need to show extra kindness by doing the chore for them. It's a lot easier to determine the difference when we take our eyes off ourselves and put them on the needs and emotions of the people around us and the situation as a whole instead of our narrow view of it.

When I began to live life without the cloud of negativity over my head, my home changed. I flat-out re-fell in love with my husband. Oh, poor Saul! Before kindness there were so many little things I would say and do that weren't kind. I was constantly harping on him about something. If he came home from work late, I was at the door waiting to hand him a small child. If he slept in on a Saturday morning, I was huffing and puffing all over the house because I was the one up early taking care of everybody. And don't even get me started about the crumbs he would leave on my clean counter after making a frozen pizza.

I felt like marriage was a burden. There were times I egotistically thought I could do it better on my own. Kindness taught me that my marriage is a blessing and my husband is a saint (after all, he puts up with me!). Humility kicked in when I realized all of the things my husband does to provide for our family. I saw his loyalty toward us with new eyes. Once I could see him as my partner, I stopped nagging and began communicating with him as a trusted friend. We were no longer on opposite teams. I stopped keeping score of who was doing more work. Saul noticed the change in my communication pattern, and peace filled our home. As an added bonus, I'd say my husband has become more verbal about his gratitude toward me and what I contribute to our family.

Our home is the place where we can set down the masks and be our authentic selves—and allow others to do the same. If you need a shift in perspective, ask yourself, *Will it matter a year from now?* or *Would this issue matter if one of us was battling a disease?* or even *Is someone in this room in need of a nap?*

The way we interact with others at home sets the tone for the rest of the day. It determines how we'll sleep at night. Thanks to the constant creation of pathways in the brain, it also determines how we will react to similar situations in the future.

If you're not happy in your home, you're not happy anywhere. Use kindness as your superpower to create a place you'll want to call home.

Questions to ponder when someone continually annoys you:

1. What can I trim from my schedule to create more space to breathe?
2. Who do I need to check in with and ask, "How are we doing?" Am I open to making the changes they may suggest?

Being Kind to People
Who Hurt You

I was one of those little girls who adored her momma. My mother was a stay-at-home mom until I was in third grade. My brother and sister are five and eight years older than me, so I got my mom to myself a lot as a small child. She would take me to the library and make yummy lemon bars for me. When Dad came home from work, the whole family would sit down at the table for dinner. I always knew I was loved.

One night when I was about eight or nine, a terrible fight broke out in our home. I had just gone to bed when the screaming and slamming and breaking began. All I remember is chaos and words I had never heard before being spewed by voices I loved but now feared.

I padded out in my jammies, looking for my older siblings. My father intercepted me and sent me back to my room. With no clue what was happening on the other side of the door, I sat on my bed and waited for it to end. Then I smelled smoke.

The window in my second-story bedroom looked down over the front concrete patio. My dad was standing there burning something while my mom shrieked from inside the house. As I looked out the window, my father looked up. Between the anger and the flames, I still remember thinking I was gazing straight into hell.

In a way, I guess I was. My father was burning love letters from my mom's boyfriend. I should have felt sorry for him; he was obviously in pain, but that moment at the window seared a fear of my father in my heart that lasted for the next decade.

When the smoke cleared, I learned my mother was moving out. She had recently gone back to work as a teacher in a men's prison about forty-five minutes from our home. It was a well-paying job, but the cost we paid as a family was higher. My mom fell in love with a prison inmate.

Since I was still in elementary school, my parents shared custody of me. My older siblings were allowed to come and go as they pleased. My sister quickly escaped to college far away, and my brother moved in with a neighbor.

Initially I spent three days a week with one parent and four days with the other. After a few years, we switched to two weeks at a time so I could keep better track of homework and clothes.

Every other Saturday, when I was with my mom, we would go visit her boyfriend in prison. As an adult, that might seem just the teeny-tiniest bit insane. As a ten-year-old, though, I thought it was the coolest thing ever. I got to do something none of my friends got to do. When I was in fourth grade, I even got to be the flower girl in my mom's prison chapel wedding.

We entered the prison through a brick building surrounded by ominous barbed wire and electric fencing. I was always fascinated by the watchtower high above the prison grounds and imagined sirens and spotlights as someone tried to make his escape.

Inside the brick building were two security checkpoints. First we walked through an arched metal detector and then the guard used a special wand to check any suspicious areas. My mom learned quickly not to wear an underwire bra on her visits because they added a lot of time in security. Once we were cleared for takeoff, we got an invisible stamp on our hands. At the end of the visit we waved our hands under a black light to reveal the most amazing shimmery, purple iridescent design. Once I had kids, I realized they also have those magic stamps at Chuck E. Cheese's. Perhaps I'm too easily impressed. At the time, it was cool, but I never wanted to wash my hands in prison because I was afraid I'd wash it off and the guards wouldn't let me out.

The best part of prison Saturdays was the vending machines. My mom would give me a roll of quarters and I could ration them out during the day on chips, candy, sandwiches, fruit, and frozen meals. Picking something frozen was a bonus, because then I got to use the microwave all by myself, which in 1985 was cutting-edge technology.

Being with my mom in the prison was awesome, until it wasn't. The older I got, the more ashamed I became because our family was so different from other families. By the time I was in eighth grade, my mom's husband was moving into a halfway house. My dad, fearing for my safety during overnight visits with my mom and her recently free husband, decided we should move too far away for joint custody. My mom agreed to let him take me. Dad and I moved two and a half hours away to Appleton, Wisconsin.

All I wanted as a teenager was a home. I wanted a home that looked like all of my friends' homes. In my mind, that meant living with a mom and a dad under the same roof, preferably a roof that did not also cover someone else's home like our duplex did. Also, I wanted a dog. But as Mick Jagger taught me, "You can't always get what you want."

My relationship with my mom disintegrated quickly. I assumed she intentionally chose a prison inmate over her daughter and basically did my best to shut her out of my life. I took that bitterness all the way into my adulthood, where it began manifesting itself through rum and cokes, cigarettes, and food. Thank goodness for that girl in fashionable boots at the mall play area that winter's day.

After meeting Dinoland Fashionista and feeling so alive from such a small act of kindness, I chased after more of those experiences. At first I just wanted to learn how to duplicate that feeling and then I became passionate about convincing other people to try it for themselves. That's why I started to write a weekly column in our local newspaper. I was pursuing kindness, and I wanted others to join me.

My pursuit of kindness unintentionally led me to a place of deep self-reflection. People would stop me in the grocery store and say, "Aren't you the lady who writes for the newspaper? You really have this kindness thing down." I even had one woman say, "I was in a tricky situation and I thought to myself, What would Nicole do?" It was all very humbling, because every time someone said something, all I could see was a big neon sign over my head that screamed, "Fraud!" I couldn't accept their compliments because I knew deep down that I still had a long way to go before I could be called *kind*.

I trained myself to extend kindness to anyone who crossed my path, except the one woman who longed for it the most: my mom. I was holding a grudge that was anything but kind. She would call and I would avoid calling her back. She would ask to come visit over the holidays and I would explain that holidays were too busy for us to have company.

I couldn't figure out how to get beyond my anger and resentment. In an attempt to overcome this toxicity, I vowed to myself that I would build a bridge of compassion. I began to look for commonalities. We were both moms. We had both known love and loss and friendship. Then I began looking for the differences. What might she have experienced in life that I couldn't understand?

I began to question things that had never occurred to me before. I wanted to know what life was like for my mom growing up. I wanted to know about her relationship with her parents. I wanted to know why she married my dad, and what their marriage was like in the days leading up to the affair. I asked her why she would follow her fling instead of fighting for her family. I asked her why she would let her teenage daughter go. I didn't ask those things as accusations; I asked from a place of true curiosity, almost like I was researching someone else's life.

The things I found out were game changers. I learned my mom had been abused in a variety of ways by her own father from the time she was very little. She had dated my dad for only six weeks before he proposed, and she said yes mainly to escape her home life. When the prison inmate slid a note to her across the table that said, "You are the most beautiful woman I have ever seen," it was like a drug to her. Days before, she'd had a fight with my father and the words were too tempting to turn down. She never intended the slope to be so slippery, to get out of control so quickly. She soon was in too deep and didn't know how to get out. When it came to giving up her daughter, my mom said she knew she wasn't making healthy decisions. She wasn't certain she could protect me and provide for me, so she put me somewhere she knew I'd be safe—with my father.

They say the truth will set you free. It set both of us free. My mom and I are very close now, and I look at her with awe and respect. The inmate got out, had an affair with a seventeen-year-old, and left my mom heartbroken and bankrupt. She lost everything. But in her fifties, she went back to school and got her master's degree, on her sixtieth birthday she ran a full marathon, and at age sixty-nine she retired and moved to Florida, where she teaches English as a Second Language and enjoys the views from the beach. She has peace in her life. We both do.

Extending kindness to a person who has deeply hurt you can be a lifetime battle. But when I've seen it done, in dysfunctional families, in contentious divorces, and even in political or religious communities, compassion has always been key.

Finding common ground or understanding for why someone acts the way they do helps us build a bridge of compassion. Even if we never agree with them, we can still lead with kindness because it comes from a place that acknowledges we are all in some way wounded.

My boys were messing with each other in Walmart the other day, and I was sicker than sick of it. *He looked at me funny. He whispered something under his breath. He started it.* Do we really need to have this conversation in the facewash aisle? Yep, apparently we do. I went on to explain we cannot control what someone else says or does, but we can control how we respond to it. And if they continued to respond in ways that annoyed their mother, they were both losing electronics. That settled things down nicely.

What about when it's not kids who are looking at us funny or saying mean things under their breath? What about when it's another adult? Or worse yet, our own overly judgmental parent? As much as we'd love to set someone in their place once and for all, we can't. We don't get to control another person's words or actions, but we do get to control ours.

I have an adult friend, Laura, whose mother has no concept of time. After years of being on pain medication, sleep eludes this mother, and she forgets people might be in bed when she picks up the phone. I suggested my friend just ignore her calls, but then I found out the mother does not like to be put through to voicemail. It becomes a tool for a guilt trip the next day. Laura said it was easier to just answer the midnight call and get it over with.

There are three Cs I like to implement with people who are awakening my inner meanie. We've talked about one of them: *compassion*. The second is *control*. Control requires setting boundaries. It gives us the power back in the relationship, because we get to decide how much foolishness we're willing to accept from another person and how much we're going to brush off.

Laura had a tough conversation with her mom and basically told her how the late-night calls disrupted her sleep schedule and therefore her productivity the next day. Laura clearly explained she loved to talk with her mom but would no longer be answering the phone after 10:00 p.m. There was some pushback and whining and guilt-giving on the part of the mom, but the message was clear. The next time the mom called at night, as tempted as my friend was to answer the call, she ignored it. The next day, when the mom complained about being sent to voicemail, Laura gently reminded her of the "no calls after ten" rule. Eventually, the mother began respecting the daughter's wishes.

I found kindness with my mother through compassion; my friend Laura found it through a recalibration of control. Unfortunately, when it comes to people who hurt us or bring out the worst in us, things don't always work out so smoothly. That brings us to the third C: *closure*.

Another dear friend of mine has endured years of abuse by her mother. Anna's parents divorced when she was a child, and as much as her father loved her, her mother seemed to despise her. Anna is on a mission to live a life defined by kindness. She is passionate about demonstrating love and compassion to her young sons, so despite her mother's total lack of interest and cutting comments, Anna continued to reach out and try to make amends.

Each interaction left Anna feeling unwanted, rejected, and just plain sad. This went on for years, until Anna finally made a decision. It was time for closure. She was done inviting her mom to the kids' birthday parties. She was done calling her on the phone and hoping for a civil response. She was done expecting a Christmas card in the mail. Anna wasn't bitter or angry, she was simply done. She knew she had to protect her heart for her husband and children, and she knew that meant having peace and closure with her mom in her own mind. It wasn't a big production. She didn't call her mom and say, "This is it! This is your last chance!" Anna just made the decision to move on.

When Anna and I talked about it, she mentioned feeling like she was giving up on kindness. I see it as exactly the opposite. I think Anna was embracing kindness by using closure to clear out room in her life for healthy, productive relationships.

How do you feel when you spend all day (or all week) wondering why someone hurt you? Do you feel invigorated? Refreshed? Ready to take on life's challenges? Nope. If you're anything like me, you feel sad, unqualified, and confused. That means when my son wants to talk about his favorite YouTuber or a new friend at school, I tune out. I don't have the capacity to engage with him because I've already used that energy on someone else. When we say yes to one thing, we are saying no to something else. Who or what do you want to be saying no to? Does the person hurting you really deserve all that attention?

Using compassion, control, and closure to deal with people who hurt us does not mean we get to live in a perfect little utopia where everyone gets along. Relationships are hard and require continual fine-tuning. Using the three Cs is transformational because they change our posture toward those difficult situations. We see people differently, we determine how much control they have in our lives, and we decide how much of ourselves we're willing to give away. We can't control someone else's words or actions but we can control ours, and that's a great place for healing.

Questions to ponder when you are determining whether or not to answer the phone at midnight:

1. Who has hurt me in the past and is still affecting my present?
2. How can I change my posture toward that situation with compassion, control, or closure?

10

When Kindness Can't Fix It

One Friday afternoon, two men in police uniforms knocked at my friend Catherine's door. Her twenty-three-year-old son, Tag, had committed suicide. A hiker found him in the woods. Catherine and her husband went with the coroner to identify Tag's body.

There are no words for some of the things that happen in life. None. When we are the bystander, we sit back and think, *How would I ever get through that?* As a friend, I want to wrap Catherine's entire family in my arms and reassure them it was all just a bad dream. I want to wave my kindness wand and make it all go away. But kindness can't fix it.

The child in school who wears her heavy winter coat all day every day because she has been sexually assaulted—I've seen her. I've talked to her. I've longed to wipe away the fear and the shame. But kindness can't fix it.

The stunningly beautiful teenager who can no longer attend school or even gather the strength to go for a walk because her mind tells her disintegrating body she's too fat to eat. She sits in a treatment center with other kids whose minds are telling them the same thing. I want to open their eyes to see what I see. But kindness can't fix it.

The woman in town who learns her husband is having an affair. He walks out the door after telling her the entire marriage was a sham, the kids were a mistake, and he never loved her in the first place. She crumbles on the floor. I want to fast-forward time so she can see herself in the arms of someone who appreciates both her strength and her gentleness, who loves her children in a way their father never could. But kindness can't fix it.

The stay-at-home mom with one child going blind, another child with cancer, and a husband who lost his job. I want to write a check to pay off the cars and the house and then hire the best specialists in the world to heal her kids. But kindness can't fix it.

I love kindness so much. I see it as a superpower, a way to create miracles in the midst of our everyday lives. But there are times when kindness can't fix it. So, what do we do? Back away in fear of adding more pain to an already difficult situation? I don't think so. I think we lean in.

I was standing in the shower, sobbing. It was the one place I could go and release the overflow of emotions coursing through my body since being diagnosed with breast cancer. My husband called from the other side of the curtain, "Honey, are you okay?"

I answered in my best everything-is-fine voice, "Yep, just taking a shower."

"Are you crying?"

"No. Go away."

Instead of leaving me there alone with my pain, my husband leaned in. Fully clothed, he stepped into the shower and pulled me into a hug.

I will never forget that day. His willingness to get soaking wet taught me an important lesson about leaning in when people are hurt. Kindness can't fix the tough stuff in life, but it can soften the hard edges and create a beautiful silver lining, so we have a place to put our eyes when sorrow tries to steal our focus.

In Catherine's situation, that meant an overflowing church and more cards than her mailbox could hold from people wanting to share their favorite Tag story. It meant a woman in town coordinating a dinner for hundreds of people in Tag's honor. It meant friends flying in from all over the United States to be there for the funeral.

For the little girl who had been a victim of sexual assault, kindness meant teachers bending the dress code rules a bit, sitting with the girl in the library when she needed a little one-on-one attention, and pairing her up with kids who were thoughtful and gentle when it came time for group activities.

For the beautiful girl with the eating disorder, kindness came in the form of friends who texted daily with all the school gossip, so she wouldn't feel so distant when she returned to class. It meant prayers for the family as they navigated the tricky minefield of food. It meant a close friend leaving little tokens of love on the front step during the roughest days of treatment.

The woman in town whose husband walked out found her calendar filled with girlfriends who wanted to take her for coffee and bring her dinner.

The stay-at-home mom with two sick kids and an unemployed husband found kindness through an entire community of people each giving what they could through gift cards, babysitting services, and washing machine repairs.

Little acts of love happen a million times a day in our world without us ever hearing about them. But some of those acts don't stay so little. Sometimes they start off small and grow to change the world.

I stand in awe of people who take their personal trauma and turn outward to help others. Imagine the grief of losing a child.

I don't think we can even begin to comprehend such loss unless we've experienced it. While I understand the power of kindness, I still don't understand the strength that emerges in some people during their darkest of times.

My girlfriend was passing the eleventh mile marker of the Nationwide Children's Hospital half-marathon in Columbus, Ohio, when she saw a #BrockStrong sign. Mile 11 is known as the Angel Mile. It's reserved to honor, remember, and celebrate the lives of children who are no longer with us.

Brock Johnson battled an unknown autoimmune disease since he was five days old. As he grew, you couldn't see from the outside how sick his body was on the inside. Surgeries, hospital stays, infusions, and transfusions couldn't stifle Brock's competitive spirit, especially when it came to baseball.

Brock was fourteen when he died from an infection. The entire community was rocked by the death of this boy who'd brought so much joy and light everywhere he went. In a collective effort, they formed the Brock Strong Foundation. The group spreads Brock's favorite message, "Every day is a gift," by sponsoring kids to play travel baseball, providing financial assistance to families at Nationwide Children's Hospital, and (my personal favorite) through an explosion of random acts of loving kindness.

Each year on Brock's birthday, Broctober 19, the group does eleven big acts of kindness (because Brock wore number 11). One year, the group showed up at a daycare center and paid for five families' bill for the week. Volunteers have taken over several drive-thru restaurants for an hour and have surprised grocery shoppers by paying for their tab at the cash register. They have even given $50 bills to people shopping at a dollar store. Brock's mom, Kristi, says they just want to make ordinary people feel important and special. She says in a world where there is so much negativity, they want to bring Brock's light and keep it going.

Jeannette Maré knows the pain of losing a child. Her three-year-old son, Ben, died in 2002 when he had a cold and his airway swelled shut. She says she probably would have died herself if it hadn't been for their six-year-old son, Matthew, who needed his parents more than he'd ever needed them before.

In an effort to incorporate coping strategies into their home, the family began working with clay in their backyard studio in Tucson, Arizona. Friends came over, and as hands were busy molding and painting, the shared stories soothed the pain and led the family to a place of healing. On the first anniversary of his death, hundreds of Ben's Bells were hung all over town with a little note attached asking people to take one home and pass on the kindness.

Jeannette says the ripple effect was amazing. She found that many people had stories to tell of hurting and healing and hope. Eventually Jeannette's family opened a hands-on art studio for the community. That was followed by several more in Connecticut and Phoenix. People come and put in their earbuds to sit alone with their thoughts or visit with others and share their stories as they work on the next step of each bell. By the time one of Ben's Bells is ready to hang, at least ten people are involved in its creation.

On December 14, 2012, Mark Barden walked his first-grade son, Daniel, to the bus stop. He hugged him and kissed him and told him he loved him. Shortly after, Mark started getting calls and texts and emails saying there was a lockdown in the district. When he got the alert there had been a shooting at Sandy Hook Elementary, he raced down to the school. He began looking for Daniel. Daniel was part of a classroom of victims killed that day.

Mark says he will carry the shock and trauma of that moment for the rest of his life. He readily admits he will never get over Daniel's death. But that doesn't mean he is sitting still in his grief. Mark is pouring his efforts into Sandy Hook Promise. The nonprofit strives to make sure this sort of tragedy never happens to another family by working with thought-holders across the country to prevent gun violence in schools. They train students and adults to look for warning signs through programs implemented in all fifty states. As of 2018, they had trained 3.5 million people.

One resident of Newtown, Connecticut, told me the culture of her town changed for the better on that terrible December day. While she would have identified Newtown as a kind community before, she says the collective hurt has drawn them together and caused community members to look out for each other more than ever.

Sometimes our pain can even bring total strangers—miles apart—together. After the Sandy Hook shooting, volunteers in Tucson sent more than one thousand Ben's Bells to Newtown. Community members eventually started their own chapter of Ben's Bells so people in Connecticut could grieve and heal together.

The tricky thing about life is that one day we can be singing and laughing and blowing out candles in a birthday celebration and the next day our entire world is set on fire. Joy and pain exist simultaneously. Those birthday celebrations often come with an empty place at the table. When our greatest fears are recognized, we have pain, but joy is quietly standing to the side, waiting for an invitation as people step forward longing to love and care for us. Joy and pain travel together. I think that's important to realize because it gives us permission to laugh in the face of adversity. Every single thing in our life can stink, but then we see a video of a dog wearing a hooded sweatshirt and we can't help but giggle. For my friends who find comfort in prayer, imagine this: on one hand we have joy, on the other we have pain. When we bow our heads to pray, we clasp our hands together, uniting the joy and pain and giving them both to God.

We can channel more of that joy in hard times by intentionally remembering other people who are also experiencing difficulties. When my friend Catherine's son died, my husband was out of a job. Her tragedy reminded me to hug my babies a little tighter. It changed my perspective on our situation. In return, Catherine told me my circumstances reminded her to give thanks for her home and her work and the other sources of stability in her life.

It's not a matter of comparing who has the harder life. When it comes down to it, if you're reading this book, someone has it worse than you do. But, yes, someone also has it better. Recognizing we're not the only ones hurting gives us the motivation to take our eyes off ourselves and see the people around us. When we can see them, we can begin to determine what they need and find ways, even in the middle of our own pain, to lean in to them and love them well. That might mean dropping off a soda for a coworker just because you know she secretly adores Mountain Dew. It might mean sending a quick text to a friend whose child just left for college. It might mean smiling at the grocery clerk, asking how she's doing, and actually waiting to hear the answer.

Kindness is like a secret pathway to healing. We enter the path by doing an act of kindness for another person, but what we realize is that, somewhere along the way, we are actually the ones receiving. It's not meant to be an exhausting mission. When we're experiencing trauma, the last thing we want to do is wear ourselves out, so please don't look at this as a rigid formula. After all, sometimes we don't need kindness; we need a nap. This isn't about quantity. It's about quality. It's about intentionally turning our eyes off ourselves and putting them on another person, so the pain for both of us is lessened.

Kindness can't turn back time. It can't undo illness or violence, but that doesn't mean we should underestimate its power. Kindness is not a fluffy, "when I feel like it" sort of concept. Kindness has teeth. When we engage it during the most terrible of times, we see healing begin in miraculous ways.

Questions to ponder when you are in the middle of a battle for your health or sanity:

1. What is one silver lining or point of joy in the midst of the pain I'm experiencing?
2. Who around me needs a bit of kindness in their own circumstances? How can I fill that need?

When Good Acts of Kindness Go Bad

Do acts of kindness ever go wrong? You betcha. How I'd love to say it all works out and everything we do makes a dramatic difference in someone's life and everyone lives happily ever after. However, things don't always work out the way we anticipate. Sometimes our offers of kindness are rejected, which makes us feel like we are rejected. Sometimes we see something wrong in another person's life and think *I can help them get back on the right path! Tah dah!* And then they end up asking us for rent money three months in a row.

I've been at this game long enough to have seen kindness work out exactly as it should—and work out exactly as it shouldn't. I'm going to get very real with you, but first, I've asked some social media friends to tell me what stops them from doing acts of kindness.

A few people said time, money, or laziness. A few others admitted to being too caught up in their own business and busyness to notice the opportunities around them.

But check out these other answers.

"The fear of my gesture being rejected or ridiculed. It has happened to me before."

"Fear holds me back from being kind. Fear that the recipient will reject whatever I'm trying to do or fear that I will help the wrong person (some guy stuck by the side of the road or someone asking for money) and they will take advantage of me or my family."

"Being made fun of is what mostly holds me back."

"Nasty people! Boy, it's hard sometimes!"

"Sometimes I am overwhelmed by the magnitude of the need. I can't fix the entire problem, so I wonder if my small gesture is worth it, or if it will commit me to more than I can handle."

"When being kind is misunderstood as something you do to try to bring attention to yourself."

"How I look and how I'll be judged by the person receiving it."

"When people continue to cause drama; when it could be harmful to others."

"Thinking my kindness is not quite big enough to make a difference."

"Second guessing or worrying that the gesture isn't good enough or just right."

I see one constant in this list: fear. We are afraid of each other. We are afraid of getting it wrong. We are afraid people will start asking for more than we can give. We are afraid of being put in an uncomfortable situation. We are afraid our little bit isn't enough.

Sometimes fear is a good thing. It's what stops me from picking up hitchhikers along the side of the road. That's not a good act of kindness for me. It might work for others, but I know it doesn't work for me.

Fear also keeps me from allowing complete strangers to sleep on my couch. Again, for some people that works. For me, not so much.

When it comes to kindness, we cannot live in a place of fear. We can feel it and acknowledge what it's trying to tell us, but then we need to make a decision.

If we're not giving to someone else because we are afraid we might look like we're trying to draw attention to ourselves, that's pride. Pride is dumb. It is absolutely possible to do an act of kindness without worrying what other people will think. I do it all the time. I don't care if people see me do the kindness or not. If they do happen to stumble upon it, then I hope they get a strong dose of those feel-good chemicals running through their bodies.

In my weekly newspaper column, I ask readers to send in stories of times they have either given or received kindness and how it made them feel. People have said, "I don't want to send in the story of an act of kindness I've done, because then I'm just bragging." You know what I say to that? Hogwash! If we don't share how great it feels to do an act of kindness, how will people ever be tempted to try it? Besides, if we don't show our friends and family that normal people can make a difference in someone's day, they might begin to believe the lie that in order for an act of kindness to help, it has to be big. That is not true.

Remember the starfish story? A little boy notices the starfish have washed up onto the beach by the thousands. He starts picking them up one by one and tossing them back into the ocean. An old man walks up and says, "What are you doing? There are thousands of starfish here. You can't possibly make a difference." The little boy calmly responds, "I can make a difference to this one."

Fellow kindness advocate Neal Nybo told me about an update to the story, in which someone else on the beach takes a video of the boy and posts it online. Within minutes, hundreds of people have gathered to help the boy throw back the starfish.

Sure, that story is fiction, but versions of it happen every day in real life. Please don't believe the lie that your act of kindness is too small to make a difference.

As far as being put in uncomfortable situations, that happens. I have hardly ever tried to buy coffee, groceries, or anything else for someone without them first saying, "Oh, no. I couldn't." It's our knee-jerk reaction to refuse someone's kindness. We've already talked about why we should be quick to say yes to kindness, but apparently the people I'm trying to buy coffee for haven't listened to any of my presentations or read any of my stuff. I forgive them. I never walk away, though, when they say no. I simply explain that I love to do an act of kindness each day, and if they'd accept this gesture they'd really be helping me out, because if they say no I have to think of a new act to do. That usually does the trick.

When you do an act of kindness for someone, there is a chance they will want more. They may very likely see you as their cash cow. You could feel like they're beginning to take advantage of you.

I could share many stories of times when my husband and I have had people take advantage of our kindness, when they've come back asking for more than we were comfortable giving. The problem is, we're still friends with those people. It would be very hurtful to some of the people in our small town if they thought we were keeping score. Because we're not.

Here are the two lessons I've learned about dealing with nasty people (or people who turn into big meanies when we tell them no) and people who just keep pushing us to the edge of our generosity.

1. Learn how to say no.
2. Don't keep score.

First, learn how to say no. Saul and I paid the rent for a family who was in danger of being evicted. We loved their children and didn't want to see them displaced. Saul and I had previously talked about our giving limits. We agreed we would help the kids with food, clothes, and rides, but we wouldn't be paying utility bills, rent, bail, or court costs should the need come up. Well, there I was, standing in front of this struggling mother who asked for $750 for rent. I stalled a bit and said since that was a big chunk of change, I really needed to talk to my husband before committing.

Saul and I agreed to help them out. I'm a bit of a bleeding heart and may have begged a bit, so my husband basically said, "Fine. But this is the only time." I went back and delivered the check to the landlord, but made sure to tell our friend that we weren't going to be able to do this particular act of kindness again.

Several months later, it was déjà-vu. A series of unfortunate events had unfolded, leaving this family with no rent money. She came back to me, and I had to say, "I'm sorry, but we can't help you." I knew she was having a hard time budgeting each month, even without these events, so I did what my husband suggested and offered to help this mother work out a monthly list of expenses so she'd know what she had to work with. She never took me up on the offer, but she also never asked for rent money again.

We are still actively involved in each other's lives. Sometimes she needs a ride to the grocery store and I can drive her, but other times I know it's in my best interest to say no. I don't feel the need to reschedule my entire day to fit in a favor or an act of kindness. I decide day by day what works for my family. I can do that because I've gotten better at letting people know I love them while also saying no.

One day my sister called me in a panic from her car. She was five states away and needed a quick kindness intervention. "This woman at the gas station just asked me for money to pay for her gas. I didn't feel right giving it to her. It just sort of felt wrong, but I don't know why. I didn't know what to tell her. What should I have done?"

To the best of my recollection, what my sister did do was buy time. She went into the gas station to use the bathroom and pay her own bill, and by the time she walked back outside, the woman was gone. But my sister was left wondering what she should have done.

I'm a big fan of following our gut instincts. When I feel my gut say *give*, I give. When I feel my gut say *no*, I say no. I could tell my sister clearly wasn't comfortable making a donation to this lady's gas fund. I told my sister what I tell people when I have to say no. I look them in the eye so they know I'm not rushed or bothered, and I let them know I truly see them and their predicament. Then I sweetly but firmly say, "I'm sorry, but that's not going to work for me today." I usually follow up with, "I hope your day goes better," or "Good luck." Then I walk away.

I also use that line when I'd rather chew my arm off than commit to some event someone wants me to volunteer for, and I use it when people ask me for time, money, or anything else I don't want to give. "I'm sorry, but that's not going to work for me today."

A US senator's wife told me once that she never commits to anything on the first ask. She always says, "I'll have to pray about that." The good news is she literally does pray about it, so it's not just a cop-out. I hate it when people do that. Be honest. Be straightforward. Take some time to think about it, and then be okay with saying no.

Surprisingly, I've never had someone get nasty and turn their inner meanie loose on me for saying no. Usually they know what they're asking for is a favor, something I'm not obligated to give, so they just move on and ask someone else. Maybe a few have gotten mad at me, but I just don't remember, which brings us to our second lesson: don't keep score.

Not keeping score means after an act of kindness is given, we let it go. We don't spend time wondering if the recipient used the money in an appropriate way. We don't count how many times they've asked us for this same favor. We don't wait for a thank-you note.

It's so hard not to keep score. I don't intentionally weigh what I've done versus what they've done, but my brain is apparently so amazing it can do it subconsciously. The other day I was buying a Christmas present for someone, just like I've done for the last five years. At that moment I realized the other woman had never, not once, given me anything in return. No gift, no thank-you note, nothing. The woman lives well below the poverty line, but I believe everyone has something to give. It could be an intentional word of encouragement, a briefly jotted note, or half a batch of homemade cookies.

There I was standing at the checkout thinking, *Why am I even buying this gift?* when I realized I was doing it because I wanted to. I liked to know we'd made her holiday a little brighter. I'm convinced my kindness matters to her whether she's able to express that to me or not.

When our brains begin to keep score, it's time to have a serious conversation with ourselves. We have to either agree to cut back on kindness so we aren't feeling used and abused, or we have to remind ourselves why we're doing the act in the first place.

I'm going to get really real with you. When you dig really deep into another person's life, the chances of having your heart broken are high.

I knew the risk factors going into a fostering situation with a teenage boy. First, he spent some time at our house and eventually decided not to go back home. His relatives could see a dramatic change in the disposition of this sad kid, so they agreed to let him stay with us. I then spent months pouring into him, reminding him of how great he is and the bright path in his future. We talked a lot about how he could create a home someday that was drug-free and drama-free. My kids became his siblings. Family vacations meant making sure there was enough room to include one more.

We went running and hiking together, and he learned to make Rice Krispie bars in my kitchen. We banged our heads together over terribly hard math homework and attended counseling sessions.

Then one day I found out he had been lying to me. (Let me pause and say that nothing bothers me more than finding out someone has lied to me. It drives me crazy. My kids know if they're caught lying, Mount Saint Mommy is going to erupt. It ain't gonna be pretty.)

After this lie he had to spend a few days back at his old house while he decided how he wanted to proceed. He agreed to come back and live under our rules. Then, a few days later, I found out he was lying again about some things that could have gotten us all into a whole lot of trouble.

That was when I had to make the hardest decision of my life. I had to send him back to his old home for good. I couldn't give him the time he needed, the homeschooling he needed, or the discipline he needed because he was still involved with disconnected members of his family who were supplying him with some dangerous ideas.

I cried. He cried. I continued to bat around the terrible feeling that I should have done more, and I still feel that way sometimes.

On the day I dropped him off, with tears in my eyes I said, "I love you unconditionally, but I cannot help you unconditionally." He and I both knew he wasn't ready to help himself, so I would be spinning my wheels in a muddy ditch by trying to make him.

I saw the text messages on his phone of people calling me all kinds of nasty names, saying this whole kindness thing was a masquerade for my real behavior. They called me crazy and a whole lot of other things. It hurt, but I couldn't defend myself because part of me wondered if they were right. I was in way over my head and had no idea what I was doing, because I had never navigated a situation like this before.

The thing is, as heartbroken as I was, I know I'd do it all over again. I had grown to love that boy as if he'd always been mine. When he smiled, something in me lit up too. It was such a joy to bring him joy. I had seven months to speak life into this boy's troubled soul. I have to believe it mattered. I have to believe someday he will want a home that is drug-free and drama-free, and he will believe it is possible at least in part because of a short-term surrogate mother who told him he could create a different life.

When you get discouraged about helping, when you feel like people will take more than you can give, when you feel like it all might blow up in your face, you're right. All those things can happen. But you're much stronger than you think. And whatever you have to give, a little or a lot, matters.

Questions to ponder when you're wiping off the sticky kitchen table for the twelfth time today:

1. What will I say the next time someone asks me for something I'm not comfortable giving? (It's important to

think this out in advance, because sometimes kindness requests sneak up on us.)

2. Are there any situations that are making me feel spiteful? How can I do a better job of not keeping score? Do I need to back away or remember why I'm doing it?

12

Why Kindness Even Matters

That freezing cold winter's day I walked into the Dinoland play area at the Fargo mall, I was just doing what I could to amuse the kids and burn off some boredom until naptime. It was an average day. An ordinary day like all the others. It never occurred to me this would be the day that defined all other days of my life.

Isn't that the truth? We never know when we wake up in the morning if this day holds anything different from any other day. That should be wonderful and exciting, but when we get to the end of the day and it felt like every other day, there can be a letdown. I think that's why our passion leaves us, why we feel like there is a missing link between our lives and the actual enjoyment of our lives. It's hard to stay excited about the mundane—work, bills, laundry, getting dinner on the table day after day. Eventually, our inner meanie comes out to play, because then at least we get to feel something that distracts us from the things that can be too painful to think about. We get some sort of up and down in our day. We get to control what we feel and maybe even tell ourselves that at least we're doing life better than the next guy.

I developed a theory back in college while watching TV in the common area of the dorm with all the other freshmen. Are you ready for my profound thought? Here it is: people need a soap opera in their lives. If you're young and you don't know what a soap opera is, think *The Bachelorette*. Same thing. In the olden days, we called them soap operas. Stick with me on this one. We humans want to feel something. We get a jolt of excitement by watching other people screw up their lives on reality TV, or by gossiping about what's happening with our coworkers, or by broadcasting what's going wrong in our lives instead of what's going right.

I'm no different. I love a good soap opera. Mine comes naturally with being a college basketball coach's wife. Each fall brings a new roller coaster of emotions that soar and sink with every win and loss, leading right up to March Madness, when we fear we're going to lose our lunch.

I bet you gravitate toward drama in some specific area of your life without even realizing it. Don't feel bad; we're in this reality show together. Let's think about what we're thinking about. Is your mind on your to-do list? Maybe you're forecasting future scenarios in which something terrible happens, or something wonderful that just has to happen doesn't happen. Or maybe your inner meanie is itching to give an opinion on something that has nothing to do with you, like why the woman who works at the coffee shop would refuse to wear a bra.

Hurry, worry, jury much? When our minds are left to wander, they head straight for soap opera land. It's not really our mind's fault. Our entire body is looking for those natural feel-good chemicals; our brain is just complying.

What if we give our bodies what they want, but on our terms? What if we create just enough of a soap opera in our lives to get those chemicals we need while allowing our minds to let go of the hurry, worry, and jury?

That, my friends, is where kindness enters the scene. The music changes key, the camera slowly pans away from the single red rose, and kindness comes into focus. We wake up in the morning, and instead of wondering how this day could possibly be any different from any other day, we know without a doubt that something special is tucked into the next few hours. Then we go and get our coffee and find the person in front of us has paid for our latte. We stand in line at the grocery store and realize we have the power to breathe life into the exhausted mom waiting behind us. We pick up a candy bar for the co-worker who has to work late and are delighted as she looks at us with total confusion and gratitude. One simple, intentional act of kindness ignites a flood of warm feelings, and we have created joy and spontaneity in our lives. We didn't have to wait for someone else to make it a good day because we've done it ourselves.

This isn't a diet plan. This isn't a monthly budget. You don't need to spend one single second planning out how to incorporate kindness into your life. You don't need a spreadsheet. You just need to wake up in the morning and decide this is the day kindness becomes the lead character in your life.

That happened for me the day I met Dinoland Fashionista. After a casual conversation at a mall playland, I knew I needed to share my resources and give her some money. As I gave her my big speech and extended the money in my hand, her body language changed ever so slightly. I'm not sure if it was confusion or suspicion or whatever else makes us fearful of strangers, but I could see it. Just barely, but it was there.

I could have bolted in that moment, knowing I was making her uncomfortable in the situation. But I stood firm, and all of a sudden I was standing on holy ground. I began with the words,

"I know we're never going to see each other again . . ." Within moments, we were both in tears, hugging one another.

I truly believed this was my one and only chance to say what I needed to say. And I was right. It had to be done in that moment.

But it wasn't the last time I would see Dinoland Fashionista.

Many months later, my husband called me from the same playland. "Nic, it's Dinoland Fashionista! She's here with her son!"

Since my husband had never actually seen her, I was confused about how he could possibly identify her.

My husband continued, "She's young and has long dark hair, and her kid is Ben's age, and she has clearly showered and she's just as sweet with her little boy as you described. It has to be her."

Saul stuck around and eavesdropped long enough to hear Dinoland Fashionista tell someone that she met with a young mom's group every Tuesday. You can bet the next Tuesday I was camped out at the playland, waiting for her.

She walked in, and I knew Saul was right. It was her. Unfortunately, I hadn't planned on what would come next. In my mind, I sort of assumed she would have been as touched by our Dinoland interaction as I was and would therefore immediately recognize me and leap to her feet in gratitude. Yeah. That didn't happen. Her eyes didn't reveal any spark of recognition. I realized I was going to have to figure out a way to approach her without sounding egotistical or completely idiotic. That's not my specialty. I could just see it: "Remember me? I'm the lady who gave you money last year! Aren't you glad to see me?"

Instead I slowly approached her and said, "Um, excuse me. This is going to sound really weird, but I think we met here at the mall last winter. Your son and my son shared Cheerios." She looked bewildered, so I continued. "Um, you told me my kids really love me and then I gave you some money."

There. It was out, and I felt beyond stupid. The memory registered though, and she said, "Oh! Right! Thank you. That was so nice of you."

The next moment I was verbally vomiting all over her shoes again. "No, no, no! I gave you a few bucks, but you changed the trajectory of my life. I went home and wrote up our story and now I write a newspaper column and I speak about kindness and I'm just so glad I got to see you again so I could thank you."

We talked some more, and I found out she was working at a boutique on the opposite side of town. She mentioned seeing my "Kindness Is Contagious" column, but never actually reading it. I got out my phone and pulled up my very first story (the one about her). As I read it to her aloud, I was a little embarrassed by the amount of times I called her a fashionista, but she laughed it off. Seeing her again and sharing this column with her might not have meant much to her, but it meant everything to me.

Sometimes, when we offer kindness, people are going to turn us down or read our intentions wrong. They might not even remember us, or they may become offended and feel like a charity case. Lead with kindness anyway. Our inner meanie would love to tell us to back off and save all the time and energy and resources for ourselves. It's self-protective, but it's also a stale, mundane way to live.

It was evident the interaction at the mall wasn't nearly as impactful on Dinoland Fashionista as it was on me, which taught me a powerful lesson about kindness that I continue to preach. Kindness isn't about them; it's about us. We can see the brokenness of this world and get determined to do something to help, but the first person healed by our efforts toward others is ourselves. Love isn't a one-way street, even if someone isn't loving us back, because when we care for others, we care for ourselves. That's another reason it's so important to say yes when someone is trying to buy you a coffee or pick up your kids from school. If

Dinoland Fashionista had said no to the money I wanted to give her or hadn't struck up a conversation with me in the first place, the effect on my life would have been minimal. It may have been an interesting day, but it wouldn't have been a life-changing day. I needed her to say yes. I'm so grateful she did, because in that moment, standing next to a T-Rex in Dinoland, hugging, with tears in our eyes, kindness changed my life.

The remedy for negativity isn't a better spouse or a bigger budget or a smaller waistline. It's a shift in attitude. It's about moving our eyes from the black dots to the white space. Instead of focusing so intently on all that's going wrong, we begin to notice what's going right. When we take our eyes off ourselves and put them on others, a strange thing happens. We unlock joy and have less stress and better relationships. We are the ones who benefit. The life we transform with kindness is our own.

Acknowledgments

This book wouldn't have happened if it hadn't been for my bestie, Andrea Coombs, so I'd better start there. Andrea, you see me more clearly than I see myself, and you're always my truth-teller, even when it hurts (like the time you told me to roll down my windows instead of buying a convertible). This book was your idea, and writing it filled me with joy, just like you knew it would. Thank you.

To my agent, Keely Boeving, at WordServe Literary, thank you for believing in my words for this book and the ones that still sit on the shelf. Thank you to each person at Baker Publishing Group who touched this book and brought it to life. What an honor to be surrounded by the best of the best. In particular, thanks to Rachel Jacobson, my acquisitions editor, for being so generous with your time and flying across the country to work out the details of each chapter. And Patti Brinks, there is a reason you are the senior art director. The lightbulb went on the moment I saw your idea for the cover!

Saul, I'm so glad we're still in this together. Jordan, Charlie, and Ben, you make me better by holding me accountable to kindness. You forgive me when I get it wrong, you giggle when mean things come out of my mouth, and you humor me when I feel the need to tell you how you could be doing it differently. We've got it good because we've got each other, Team Phillips.

There are several spectacular women who keep the kindness ship afloat. Teresa South, Sarah Tachon, and Andrea Theis (and let's not forget our original team member, Amanda Koenecke), thank you for jumping in on emails, making sure I get to the next place I'm going, and believing in this message. I am so grateful to each of you, and your husbands, for sacrificing so much time on my behalf.

365 Kindness Ideas

Need some help starting your own kindness journey? While I think it's more fun just to see a need and spontaneously meet it, these quick ideas will help you train your eyes to see the kindness around you so it becomes second nature.

1. Bring a fresh hot chocolate or lemonade from a drive-thru to a parking attendant when going to an event.
2. Pay the toll of the vehicle behind you at a tollbooth.
3. Make some unexpected cookies for some kiddos just because.
4. Bring an advisor, boss, or coworker an unexpected favorite fast-food drink.
5. Send a note to your pastor's wife saying how much you appreciate all *she* does and her prayers.
6. Tell the person at the drive-thru window that you want them to personally keep your change if they are allowed.
7. Leave a favorite book at a B&B to share with the owner and guests.

8. Pick up your hardworking mate at work as a surprise and drive to get dessert.

9. Ask your doctor at your next appointment how he or she is doing. They may be surprised!

10. Offer to walk a neighbor's or friend's dog if he or she is busy, sick, or stressed.

11. Bring used jigsaw puzzles and magazines to assisted living or retirement home residents.

12. Donate your used books to the local library for others to use.

13. Offer to take care of the difference when someone in front of you at the checkout is short on cash.

14. Stock up a food pantry with all the "buy one get one free" specials at the grocery store. This makes for a fun grocery trip!

15. Fill up a cute bag with back-to-school items and give it to a teacher as extras to have on hand.

16. Offer a ride to someone having a hard time working out the details of their life.

17. Drop off old blankets/pillows for the animals at the Humane Society.

18. Donate stuffed animals to local first responders to give to children who are afraid when they're first at the scene.

19. Donate kids' pants and new underwear to your local elementary school for kids who get their clothes wet in the winter or have an accident at school.

20. Call the school lunch program and put money toward negative lunch accounts.

21. Write something you are grateful for on a pumpkin every day in November.

22. Take pictures of your friend's kids at a school concert, field trip, or soccer field, and send them to your friend.
23. Stop by a laundromat and leave laundry pods or quarters by the machines.
24. Carry a pack of sticky notes in your purse and write notes to encourage, thank, or compliment someone. Leave "You are beautiful" on a mirror, "Thank you for my favorite coffee" on the money you give at the drive-thru, or "Thank you for being an awesome mail carrier" on your outgoing mail.
25. Think of an influential person in your life and write them a gratitude letter.
26. Give plastic flags to veterans at the nursing home for Veterans Day.
27. Leave Valentine's Day cards in secret spots to remind people they are loved.
28. Stop and pick up litter on the ground.
29. Write a note on your restaurant receipt that says, "Thank you for being a fantastic server."
30. When you are in a checkout lane, look the cashier in the eyes and ask them how their day is going.
31. Next time you are getting take-and-bake pizza, order an extra one and surprise someone with dinner.
32. When you have an extra fifteen minutes, pick up an inflated Mylar balloon that says "Thinking of you," and leave it at someone's mailbox or office chair.
33. Leave extra quarters on top of the little toy machines outside stores to surprise the next kids who beg their parents to buy something.
34. Call in to your local radio station to give a kindness shout-out to someone you know, or thank the radio hosts for playing great music.

35. When you are driving and see a runner on the side of the road, give them a thumbs-up out the window.

36. Email your coworker's boss and tell him or her how much you enjoy working with your coworker.

37. Think about a loved one you have lost. Reach out to someone else who was close to them and share a story that reminds you of them.

38. Do you know someone who has given up alcohol? Send them a text and let them know you are proud of them.

39. Buy some bubbles and chalk for an emergency women's shelter.

40. Send an email or text to a friend with just emojis that make you smile.

41. Invite a friend or neighbor to go for a walk.

42. Drop off baked goods or donuts to local police officers or firefighters.

43. Send a thank-you note to your family's doctor, dentist, or pastor.

44. Add a message to the bottom of your email signature that says, "Kindness Is Contagious," "Kindness Matters," "Be Brave, Be Kind, Be You," or similar.

45. When you see someone in military uniform, make eye contact, smile, and thank them for their service.

46. Bring your auto mechanic a kindness magnet.

47. Fill a couple of cute pouches with pads/tampons and donate to the school nurse at a local middle school.

48. When you encounter an elderly person, ask if they would like help getting down the stairs or into a car. Open the door or hold their elbow.

49. If someone is carrying something really heavy, hold the door open for them.

50. Drop off ice cream or specialty cheese to a friend in a rehab center.

51. Sign up for a 5k with a good cause and do it in honor of someone.

52. Grow your hair out and donate it (usually seven inches or more).

53. Offer to drive home someone else's child from a birthday party.

54. Drop off new Play-Doh for sick kids in the hospital.

55. Leave packets of hot chocolate in the teachers' lunch room or office break room.

56. Think about the last book you loved and share it with a friend.

57. Look for someone who seems sad and ask them how their day is going.

58. Tell your parents you love them and share a favorite childhood memory.

58. Mail a care package to someone out of town.

60. Volunteer to read with kindergartners.

61. Refuse to get down on yourself when you make a mistake.

62. Drop off a basket of fresh fruit to a small business owner.

63. Leave a box of Band-Aids in the park bathroom above the paper towels.

64. Leave your spouse a love note above the toilet.

65. Say hi to the next new person you see.

66. Ask someone what their favorite food is.

67. Ask someone where they would want to go on vacation if they could pick anywhere and why.

68. Help a neighbor with yard work or snow removal.

69. Have your kids leave encouraging messages on other kids' lockers with messages like, "Thank you for being YOU!" "You are special," "Enjoy today," "Smile," "I'm so happy you exist," or "Consider this a paper hug."

70. Pay for a meal at a restaurant for someone totally unaware and leave before they do.

71. If you usually text, pick up the phone; if you usually pick up the phone, invite the person over so you can talk face-to-face.

72. Use Facebook to find out upcoming birthdays and send a card or leave a balloon.

73. Take the time to "fluff" your messages with an extra bit of thoughtfulness.

74. Buy McDonald's gift cards and give them to the homeless.

75. If you are a gardener or have access to beautiful flowers, bring a bouquet to an elderly neighbor.

76. Buy lots of colorful stickers and keep them in your purse to distract a fussy child.

77. Leave a pack of baby wipes and an extra diaper at the changing table in the public restroom.

78. Record a funny joke with audio and send it to a friend.

79. If you have a plant that produces clippings, start new plants for friends and leave them by their front doors.

80. Think about other people's hobbies, and when you have a question in this area, text them to "ask an expert."

81. Make friendship bracelets and give them away.

82. Send a text to friends struggling with infertility to let them know you are thinking of them on Mother's Day and Father's Day.

83. Spend ten minutes on Facebook liking and commenting on friends' posts instead of just checking your own.

84. Think about an area you can clean/organize to surprise your roommate or significant other (car, bathroom drawer, garage).

85. Let the kids play restaurant and serve you dinner.

86. Sit down and play a board game with your kids or parents.

87. Enjoy a sunrise or sunset with someone you love.

88. Start a fund-raiser for a charitable cause that tugs at your heart.

89. If you usually say yes to all requests for help/favors, be kind to yourself and say no this time.

90. If you usually say no to everything, pause to see if this time you could say yes.

91. When you hear an ambulance siren, take a moment to think of the people in need of assistance and the emergency response team coming to their aid (if prayer is your thing, send up a prayer for them).

92. Send a handwritten note to someone letting them know you are thinking of them.

93. Walk dogs at an animal shelter once a week.

94. Bring up the garbage bins on garbage day for people who are elderly or gone for the day.

95. Give a hug.

96. Give a high five.

97. Sincerely thank people who wait on you or serve you.

98. Let someone go in front of you while driving or shopping.

99. Help people unload their cart.

100. Bring a shopping cart back for someone.

101. Offer housecleaning (tub, toilet, sinks) to someone undergoing cancer treatment.

102. Be the one to organize a meal train for a hurting family.

103. If you are hosting the holidays, invite someone who may be alone.

104. Make a pot of spaghetti sauce for someone who needs a break, such as a single parent or working student.

105. Give a gas gift card to someone who has to drive to doctor's appointments.

106. Give pizza or a gift card to a volunteer kids' coach.

107. Leave a plant for the families of those you see in the newspaper obituaries.

108. Send a card.

109. Give a May Day basket.

110. Paint rocks and leave them in fun places for people to find.

111. Deliver a batch of caramel rolls to your neighbor on Christmas morning.

112. Send someone a "thanks for being you" note, even if they haven't given anything to you or done anything for you.

113. Leave flowers on a stranger's gravesite.

114. Leave money in a vending machine for someone to use.

115. Pay it forward at a coffee shop or restaurant!

116. Go to Target and hand out $5 gift cards.

117. Offer to hold or talk to a crying baby for a frazzled mother when she is going through the checkout aisle.

118. Pick up Dairy Queen Dilly Bars and bring them to the office when you know it's going to be a "Dilly of a Day!"

119. Volunteer at a local homeless shelter.

120. Rather than having that big rummage sale, give everything to a thrift store.

121. Send a thank-you note to the people who help you unload at the thrift store and let them know what they do is important because it gives to others and saves our landfills.

122. Hand out random $2 bills and tell people "You are TWO nice!"

123. Put together Ziploc gift bags for people who are homeless. Include $1 in quarters, individual packets of laundry detergent, a toothbrush and toothpaste, a comb, a bar of soap, a granola bar, a washcloth, and so on. Hand them out to the people you see on the side of the road with homeless signs.

124. Invite people to your home.

125. Have a "free" rummage sale. Don't take a dime but have a conversation with the people who come, asking them to share what they intend to do with their selections.

126. Host a pink flamingo potluck in your neighborhood. Send out a flyer to the people on your block and tell them they are invited to your pink flamingo party. They will get a reminder the morning of the party on their way to work because you will put up pink flamingos in your yard early in the day.

127. Pick up garbage lying around in the park you frequently visit.

128. Befriend an elderly person from your church. Invite them for dinner, take them to the grocery store, or just listen to their story.

129. Secretly find out the name of someone at church or school who is in need. Gather gift cards, small gifts, or

books and put together a care package. Leave it anonymously on their porch.

130. Buy lemonade from kids and leave a nice tip.
131. Use your rewards from a loyalty card to buy something for someone else.
132. Buy several dozen donuts and hand them to the people flagging during construction. Thank them for working in all weather conditions and dealing with angry drivers.
133. Give the local school crossing guard a light for foggy conditions or a big flag, and tell them thank you for keeping our kids safe while crossing the road.
134. When you see a baby, tell the parent they have a beautiful baby, no matter what you may really think.
135. Put a note in your calendar each week to call an older relative who lives alone.
136. Compliment an airline person, saying they have cool earrings, a beautiful complexion, or a great smile.
137. On rainy days, let someone else have your umbrella.
138. Drop off cards of encouragement at a nursing home or hospital.
139. Offer to pump gas for a stranger on a cold, wet, or windy day.
140. If you like an outfit, jewelry, shoes, or haircut, tell the person.
141. When you see a kid doing something nice or good, give them a pat on the back.
142. Tell someone who really needs it that they're doing a great job.
143. Deliver for Meals on Wheels.
144. During the Christmas season, give out small, handmade ornaments to clerks as you go through their checkout line during your holiday shopping.

145. Invite a new neighbor to go with you to your local Fourth of July parade.
146. Write welcome notes for lockers at school or doors at your college's residence halls.
147. Put signs on the roads near schools that say "Teachers rock!" or "We love our teachers."
148. Drop off flowers or a small gift for Hospice workers.
149. The next time you have to drive 30–60 minutes somewhere, call a friend or acquaintance to ride along. They may need a listening ear.
150. At church, seek out someone who may look a little lost. Introduce yourself and others.
151. If you're thinking about how awesome someone is, tell them!
152. Do the dishes when it's someone else's turn.
153. Leave an ice-cream cake in a friend's driveway in the middle of winter.
154. Donate five nice things you no longer wear.
155. Give a fresh, warm blanket to someone who is homeless.
156. Compliment the first person you see in the morning, both at home and at work.
157. Text your hairdresser to tell him or her how much you like your recent cut.
158. Carry suckers or stickers in your pocket for kids.
159. Volunteer with your family at a food pantry.
160. Be the house that gives awesome candy at Halloween.
161. In new situations, look for someone who seems more uncomfortable than you and strike up a conversation.
162. Buy a soda for a friend.

163. Take bottles of water to the construction crew in your neighborhood.

164. Send an email to a former teacher.

165. Send an email to your child's current teacher.

166. Buy an extra coupon book from your town's youth sports organization for a neighbor.

167. Buy cookies (perhaps from the Girl Scouts) and give them to a men's homeless shelter.

168. Make a double batch of dinner and share with someone who hates to cook.

169. Ask the local fire department when you can bring over a meal.

170. Stock an elementary classroom with crackers or cereal for snack time.

171. Pay for a veteran's meal.

172. Host a "party with a purpose" and ask guests to bring $10 for a local charity.

173. Take pop can tabs to the Ronald McDonald House.

174. Smile at someone who looks lonely.

175. Pay for someone's birthday cake order on your birthday.

176. Go camping with your kids in the living room.

177. Give $1 to a child at a garage sale.

178. Shovel the sidewalk a little farther than you have to.

179. Bring flowers to your favorite barista, bank clerk, or gas station attendant.

180. Buy a pool pass for a family with a lot of kids.

181. Play with the neighbor's kids.

182. Keep your mouth shut when you want to retaliate.

183. If you're the boss, take coffee to your assistant.

184. Give someone your cart at the airport so they don't have to pay to rent their own.

185. Go to a nursing home and brighten someone's day by listening to their stories.

186. Look for those who need a friend and befriend them.

187. When you see something that makes you think of someone, gift it to them.

188. Help a Girl Scout meet her goal by buying as many cookies as you can afford.

189. Be the person in the stands who only says positive things when they cheer.

190. Pick up something that someone else dropped.

191. Go for a walk and bring a garbage bag to pick up litter.

192. Bring a friend a flower just because.

193. Take the time to send a happy birthday video to someone.

194. Give someone else the last cookie.

195. Donate old books to a new family.

196. Offer to babysit for parents who need to run some errands.

197. Speak up for someone who is having a hard time speaking up for themselves.

198. Wink at a stranger!

199. Hold the elevator door for people.

200. Park farther away from the door so someone else can park closer.

201. Say good morning to ten people you don't know.

202. Wave to your neighbors, even if you don't know them.

203. Carry a dry-erase marker to write positive messages on mirrors in public bathrooms.

204. Give someone your seat on a bus, plane, or subway.

205. Brush off an unhelpful or rude comment.

206. Eat lunch with someone new.

207. Pay for someone's golf balls at the driving range.

208. Send a care package to a soldier deployed overseas.

209. Help someone who is moving.

210. Give beds to families who are sleeping on the floor.

211. If you have air conditioning, invite someone in to sit and visit on a hot day.

212. Invite someone over to watch the big game when you know they don't have the channel.

213. Give mittens to the school for kids who forgot theirs.

214. Buy cleats for a young person playing baseball, soccer, or football.

215. Place an unexpected note on someone's desk.

216. Get certified to be a foster family and open your home to a child in need.

217. Cancel your plans so you can help someone at the last minute.

218. Send a hurting friend a cute box of facial tissues.

219. Thank your partner for putting the kids to bed or helping around the house.

220. Join a prison ministry group and go visit with the inmates.

221. Tip your server a little more than necessary.

222. Leave only positive messages on social media.

223. Plant a tree.

224. Plant flowers in your front yard to cheer up the neighborhood.

225. Be a temporary foster home for an adoptable pet.

226. Offer to take a friend's pet while they're on vacation.

227. Leave a positive review for a local business.

228. Recycle your magazines to a friend.

229. Refuse to think negative thoughts about yourself for one whole day.

230. Anonymously deliver pumpkins to every doorstep in your neighborhood.

231. Put your loose change in a jar each day and then donate it when you hear of a need.

232. Take pizza and paper plates to someone on moving day.

233. Wave to other drivers on the road.

234. Tidy your hotel room before you check out.

235. Vow not to complain about anything for twenty-four hours.

236. Tell someone a joke.

237. Leave a surprise note or gift card in a library book.

238. Ask your kids to forgive you when you lose your temper.

239. Admit when you are wrong.

240. Let someone use your sunscreen or bug spray at a Little League game.

241. Wear a funny hat to make other people smile.

242. Watch the movie/read the book someone suggested, then call and thank them.

243. Help a friend with their job résumé and be encouraging.

244. Visit a nursing home and offer to write letters to loved ones for them. There is a lot they want to say, but many can't write anymore.

245. Make peanut butter and jelly sandwiches and hand out in an area where you know there are people who are homeless.

246. Think of someone who might want their nails painted (friend, elderly woman, or child). Call them and tell them you want to do this for them.

247. High school teachers often get forgotten for school supplies. Stock them up with tissues, individually packaged snacks, pencils, and pens.

248. Send extra field trip money in to the office for the family that may forget or can't afford it.

249. Make your favorite baked good and mail it in a clear container to someone for fun.

250. Record yourself singing "Happy Birthday" and send it to a friend, or leave it on their voicemail.

251. Visit a local animal shelter and soak in the kindness. Find a way that tugs at your heart to help (adopt, volunteer, say an encouraging word to staff, send a letter).

252. Take a friend's vehicle through a car wash.

253. Bring extra bags for kids to catch candy at a parade.

254. Hand out "You Are Awesome" stickers with your candy to trick-or-treaters.

255. Make friends with someone who works at your grocery store. Look for them when you are shopping and learn about them. (For example, ask what their favorite type of candy is and bring it to them the next time you shop. This idea can also work for your nurse, dentist, or teacher.)

256. Write a product recommendation and send it to your favorite company.

257. Keep inspirational stickers in your car and look for opportunities to use them.

258. Join a support group.

259. Ask your neighbor about gardening/mowing tips and compliment their yard.

260. Invite a new person over to cook with you.

261. Turn your phone off for the weekend and tell your family you are doing this to focus on them.

262. Be kind to yourself. Carve out free time and schedule rest into your calendar.

263. Try a fun new craft with your kids such as making slime or puppy chow. Don't worry about the mess.

264. Think about a favor you can do for someone *today* and do it.

265. Lend out something you have that someone else may want to borrow.

266. Donate items to places that could really use them (old eyeglasses to the Lions Club, costume jewelry to Dress for Success, pajamas to a domestic abuse shelter).

267. Leave a positive Amazon review.

268. Write a letter to your favorite author.

269. Leave a cute plant or decoration in the office bathroom.

270. Give a car wash gift card to someone with a really nice car.

271. Buy a bag of sand toys and leave it at your neighborhood park.

272. Find a local "Pay It Forward" social media site to share unused items with those in your community.

273. Help local high school students think of creative community service hour ideas and implement them.

274. Surprise your kids and say yes the next time you are ready to automatically say no.

275. Mentor someone.

276. Use your influence to help someone else get ahead.

277. Run errands with a friend.

278. Let someone use your phone charger.

279. Greet your mail carrier by name.

280. Help a friend redecorate a room.

281. Compliment someone on their tattoo and ask what it means.

282. Slow down everything you're doing.

283. Tell a mom or dad what a great job they are doing.

284. Show "pre-appreciation" and give a tip before the service is done.

285. Look for a heart-shaped rock and mail it to someone.

286. Tell an older lady she has really nice skin and find out what she uses for skin care.

287. Wear a T-shirt with an inspirational kindness message.

288. Suggest your favorite restaurant, car wash, or dog groomer to someone new in town.

289. Show others their time matters by being on time.

290. Ask a little girl wearing nail polish what her favorite color is and why.

291. Help someone who is obviously struggling to read a label or find an item in the grocery store.

292. Form a kindness club at a school and help kids mentor other kids.

293. Tell a child with glasses you like their glasses and that they are cool.

294. Drop off bananas or other fruit at the teachers' lounge.

295. Ask your kids to do a singing, dancing, science presentation, magic, or other "performance" for you. Make them feel like superstars.

296. Explore nature with someone you love. Look for tadpoles, caterpillars, and other creatures.

297. Tape a dollar to a vending machine.

298. Leave a quarter in the gumball machine for the next customer.

299. Ask Grandma what her favorite cookie is, then ask to make some with her.

300. Take Grandpa to get his favorite ice cream.

301. Give Grandma and Grandpa a call out of the blue, just because.

302. Ask Mom what her favorite childhood movie was. Find it and watch it together.

303. Take your spouse's car to the car wash as a surprise for them.

304. Bring a dog lover's dog a treat the next time you see them.

305. Give your extra 20 percent off coupon to the next person in line.

306. Give someone who doesn't have a spouse a hug.

307. Send a card to "shut-ins" or people who are homebound.

308. Drive a friend to medical appointments.

309. Plan and oversee a freezer meal project.

310. Coordinate a sack lunch meal for the community in addition to local food pantry or church meals.

311. Wash windows and clean gutters for someone who cannot do it themselves.

312. Lend your trailer to someone who is moving.

313. Help a neighbor with their landscaping.

314. Pay for someone's date night or offer to babysit their kids.

315. Leave an inspirational message on the steering wheel of a teenage driver's car.

316. Lend kids' toys to grandparents who have grandchildren visiting.

317. Go visit Great-Grandma and bring her cut flowers.

318. Greet someone by their name.

319. Compliment and show appreciation to a person who bugs you.

320. Go to a visitation and wait in line to pay your respects, even if you don't know anyone.

321. Invite a college student over to do their laundry in your washing machine.

322. Order a pie from a local bakery and give it away.

323. Be the first to say "I'm sorry."

324. Put yourself in someone else's shoes to understand where they are coming from in a disagreement.

325. Ask someone to tell you their story.

326. Learn about the five love languages.

327. Ask your kids "what else" when they are crying or having a tough time so they know you want to listen.

328. Make the first five minutes when your spouse gets home intentional and positive. Stop what you are doing, greet them, and ask about their day.

329. Listen to a friend's current concern and text a few days later to check in and get an update.

330. Buy a balloon for someone you barely know on their birthday.

331. Tell your friend/coworker who is quiet and introverted what you notice about them and ask them for advice.

332. Be inquisitive about someone else's area of interest. Ask questions.

333. Write a "You are awesome!" message on a friend's car with window markers.

334. Go the extra step above and beyond what is expected.

335. Say yes and go to the Mary Kay party that you really don't want to just to support the person who invited you.

336. Make breakfast for dinner. Let the kids pile their pancakes with whipped cream, sprinkles, and chocolate chips.

337. Send a sympathy card to a couple who has a miscarriage that says "I hope you can find the rainbow at the end of your clouds."

338. Spark an atmosphere of crazy fun kindness by filling a coworker's cubicle with forty balloons on their fortieth birthday.

339. Write "Kindness Is Contagious" in chalk on the sidewalk in front of a school.

340. Share a simple act of kindness someone has done for you on social media.

341. Hold hands with your spouse, kids, or an elderly friend.

342. After someone you don't know well shares a heartwarming story, ask if you can give them a hug.

343. Buy a fun or funky lanyard for the gym teacher at your local school.

344. When you see someone stuck by the side of the road, stop and ask if they need help.

345. Bring a bag of lollipops to restock the stash at the bank, hairdresser, or anywhere else they hand them out for free.

346. Get a birthday gift for a friend's child even if you aren't going to the birthday party.

347. When the mail carrier brings a package to your doorstep, offer them bottled water or a cookie from the tray you just baked.

348. Ask for the manager at a restaurant and let them know your server did a fantastic job.

349. Leave a positive review online for your hairdresser.

350. Let your mother-in-law know you are thinking about her today.

351. Pull weeds with your neighbor when you see them outside.

352. When you hear a song that makes you think about someone, look it up and share it with them.

353. Make a mental list of things you like about a person who annoys you.

354. Allow the little girl behind you in line for the restroom to go ahead of you.

355. Give the custodian at school or church a big praise and a sweet treat for all they do.

356. When clearing your snowy driveway, use your equipment to clear a neighbor's driveway as well.

357. Water a neighbor's flowers while they are on vacation, whether they asked you to or not.

358. Mow a neighbor's or a friend's yard while they are on vacation as a nice surprise when they get home.

359. When you come across someone who wants to tell you their life situation, take a minute and really listen.

360. Pick up your spouse at work by surprise and take him or her on an impromptu dinner date.

361. Give someone new to the area a list of all your favorite places, with addresses and phone numbers.

362. Start a small weekly book club or coffee gathering in your home.

363. Call Mom or Dad today; they may be waiting to hear from you. (Even if you spoke to them yesterday.)
364. Go for a walk regularly with a friend or family member and listen.
365. Spend time with a "difficult" person and ask about their childhood.

Author Q & A

Q: How has kindness changed you?

Nicole: I was sitting in a Caribou Coffee working on this book when I noticed the daily question the barista had written on the chalkboard. It asked, "When did your life change for the better?" It almost made me cry. I can pinpoint the exact day. It was the cold winter's day a totally put-together young mom in a mall play area told me she could see my kids loved me. In exchange, I wanted to make her day a little brighter too. I learned what it feels like to pull my eyes off myself and put them on another human. That was the day I changed for the better. Everything fell into place when I began to look at myself as a vessel for love instead of just a person wandering around this planet. My husband teases me about being an updated version of the woman he married, like Nicole 2.0. It didn't come overnight, but when I committed to kindness, things definitely changed.

At first, I was intentionally looking for other people's stories of kindness so I could share them in the newspaper. Then I realized how fun it was to create my own! I went from a "me me me" mentality to someone who began to care more about what others were feeling and how I might be able to brighten their day. I started to give the compliments that popped into my head and held back the words that could be hurtful. I saw the good in people who used to annoy me. I began talking about issues instead of gossiping about people. I found an end to self-medicating and pity parties. I gained the ability to see things from a multitude of perspectives and through a lens of gratitude. I'm not always happy, but I can find the joy in each day. That's the biggest change.

Q: How have your kids benefited from your kindness journey?
Nicole: My kids were little when I struggled with addiction, so they only know what they've heard me say about it. They have a hard time visualizing me as anything but the mom they see now, who is constantly rattling on about kindness. I know they are growing up in a household that is drama-free with parents who respect each other, thanks to my break from self-medicating and the life change created by kindness. I feel good about that.

My kids are like any other kids. Sometimes they get it right, sometimes they get it wrong. That's good because it teaches them which one feels better (and kindness always feels better!). We are very intentional about looking for the kindness around us. I ask them each day about an act of kindness they participated in or witnessed. When we see people acting unkind, we talk through it, imagining what could be going on in a person's life that would make him or her act that way.

Humility and honesty cover a multitude of sins. When I'm too abrupt with my kids, I've learned to apologize and explain that I'm frustrated, hungry, or tired, so they don't think my attitude is a reflection of them. I think it teaches them to see how our feelings can overpower our words if we let them.

Q: What advice do you have for the times when we lose it and are embarrassed by our unkindness (and does that still happen to you)?

Nicole: Uh, yes. All the time. It happened most recently when I was discussing our phone plan with a representative at the AT&T store. I was getting frustrated because I wasn't getting what I wanted, and my words were getting sharper by the minute. As we sat and waited for something to update on my phone, the employee asked what I do for a living. I was mortified to tell her I write and speak about kindness. I had to admit to her that I'm a work in progress! She was gracious enough to giggle and then began to share her own story of kindness. We ended up having a great conversation, and I left the store smiling.

Q: Where do you find it hardest to be kind?
Nicole: Ugh! When I see others being treated unkindly. I hate that. It makes me want to throat punch somebody. I was in a Subway restaurant with my kids the other day when a man was totally going off on the teenage employee because his call-in order wasn't ready. She was nearly in tears as she tried to explain that her manager was in the process of fixing it. He stomped out of the store, but the bad feelings remained. When I got up to the counter, I learned my large order was also not ready. Thanks to the bad example of the man in front of me, I was reminded to keep my calm. I talked with the manager, and we worked it out. I made a point of telling her how great her employees were handling the situation—loudly, so the employees could hear the compliment.

Q: Any other thoughts you want to share with us?
Nicole: Yes! If you are in a book club or Bible study, I'd love it if you'd let this message be the catalyst to go out and do something kind either individually or as a group. Keep each other accountable and help continue to close that gap between living life and loving life by checking in each month and sharing your favorite acts of kindness. Hearing about kindness puts us in a good mood,

and it helps create a safe environment where we can be honest and vulnerable with each other.

Please share your kindness stories with me at info@nicole jphillips.com. I love to hear how kindness is transforming your world!

Notes

Chapter 2 Identifying Your Inner Meanie

1. Barbara Hirsh, *Live Kinder: Change Your Life, Your Relationships and the World* (Scotts Valley, CA: CreateSpace, 2016), 7–8.

Chapter 3 What Actual Experts Are Saying about Kindness

1. Christine Carter, *Raising Happiness: Ten Simple Steps for More Joyful Kids and Happier Parents* (New York: Ballantine, 2011), 30.

2. Christopher Hooten, "Website Reports Only Good News for a Day, Loses Two Thirds of Its Readers," *Independent*, December 5, 2014, https://www.independent.co.uk/news/world/europe/website-reports-only-good-news-for-a-day-loses-two-thirds-of-its-readers-9905916.html.

3. "Mister Rogers' Neighborhood: Look for the Helpers," YouTube video, 0:35, uploaded by PBS Kids on March 20, 2017, https://www.youtube.com/watch?v=cyOLq6tslnU.

4. Good News Network, https://www.goodnewsnetwork.org.

5. *Morning Smile*, Inspire More, https://www.inspiremore.com/morning-smile/.

6. Barb Schmidt, homepage, https://barbschmidt.com; see also https://www.facebook.com/PeacefulBarb and https://www.instagram.com/peaceful_barb/.

Chapter 4 Drawing More Kindness into Your Life

1. "Sticks and Stones," Wikipedia, accessed January 26, 2020, https://en.wikipedia.org/wiki/Sticks_and_Stones.

Chapter 5 What Counts as Kindness

1. Lysa TerKeurst, *The Best Yes: Making Wise Decisions in the Midst of Endless Demands* (Nashville: Thomas Nelson, 2014).

Chapter 7 When Kindness Isn't about You

1. Tammy Joy Lane, homepage, http://www.yestokindness.com.
2. Tammy Joy Lane, personal communication with author, used by permission.

Nicole Phillips is a champion for using kindness to overcome all of life's difficulties, including her own battle with breast cancer. She spreads the message of the healing power of kindness as host of the weekly show *The Kindness Podcast* and through her weekly column, "Kindness Is Contagious," which runs in newspapers in North Dakota and Minnesota. She is also the author of the books *Kindness Is Contagious* and *Kindness Is Courageous*.

Nicole is married to her childhood sweetheart, Saul, who is a college men's basketball coach. They have three children and a very snuggly Golden Doodle named Dakota. Nicole would love for you to share your kindness stories with her for future publication at info@nicolejphillips.com or by recording your story on *The Kindness Podcast* hotline at (701) 428-1122.

Get to Know
Nicole!

LEARN MORE AT
NicoleJPhillips.com